D0180307

mating in captivity

mating in captivity

[a memoir]

Helen Zuman

SHE WRITES PRESS

Copyright © 2018 by Helen Zuman

All rights reserved. No part of this publication may be reproduced, distributed, or transmitted in any form or by any means, including photocopying, recording, digital scanning, or other electronic or mechanical methods, without the prior written permission of the publisher, except in the case of brief quotations embodied in critical reviews and certain other noncommercial uses permitted by copyright law. For permission requests, please address She Writes Press.

Published 2018
Printed in the United States of America
Print ISBN: 978-1-63152-337-3
E-ISBN: 978-1-63152-338-0
Library of Congress Control Number: 2017955354

For information, address:
She Writes Press
1563 Solano Ave #546
Berkeley, CA 94707

Interior design by Tabitha Lahr

She Writes Press is a division of SparkPoint Studio, LLC.

For Gregg. For all who lived at Zendik.

Author's Note

I'VE SEWN THIS TEXT FROM the frayed cloth of memory, striving, per Tristine Rainer's advice, to "tell the whole truth with love."

The following are pseudonyms: Eile, Zylem, Karma, Estero, Rebel, Dymion, Prophet, Lyrik, Toba, Eave, Cayta, Zeta, Shure, Loria, Swan, Kro, Owen, Teal, Rayel, Luya, Jayd, Zar, Donna, Taridon, Riven, Blayz, Vera, Rave, Mar, Rook, Amory, Tarrow, Eric, Lysis, Noi, Dylan, Elfdancer, Mason, Ethik, Leah, Adam, and Hunter.

Contents

Prologue

I SPENT MOST OF MY twenties trapped in a story. Here it is:

You—all of you—belong to the Deathculture. You wake up, paste on fake smiles, scurry off to "work" for your corporate masters, raping the earth. You hate this, but you're stuck. You need the cash. For what? McMansions, gadgets, drugs—substitutes for love.

I belong to Zendik. *We're* starting a revolution. We live on a farm and do lots of art. We work together, support each other. Tell the truth. You've gotta follow our lead—if we're gonna save the earth.

I know—it's hard. Out there you don't *dare* get straight, even with your mate. You might lose your shield. Your one ally in your fight to survive. *Real* love takes a tribe—led by the first couple in history to do away with lies.

I'll never leave Zendik. If I did, I'd die—in soul, if not in body. And I'd despise myself, for betraying all life.

In other words, I joined a cult. The year was 1999; I was twenty-two. But I didn't say, "I joined a cult" till 2005—more than six years later.

No one knowingly joins a cult, and no one in a cult would call it that. We join, we commit to communes, new religions, personal-growth programs, temples, revolutions. Saying, "I joined a cult" comes later, if ever. It means releasing stories we doubt we can live without. Stories that give us purpose. Stories we can't see as stories, so long as they absorb us.

When I left Zendik, in 2004, I took its trap with me; I was doomed, I thought, unless I returned. What finally freed me was the only thing that ever frees anyone from mythocaptivity: a more compelling story.

[chapter 1]

Interview

I BEGAN SPINNING A FANTASY about Zendik mating the night I arrived.

Cross-legged on the living room floor, a metal bowl nestled in my lap, I watched a short, round woman with buoyant ringlets burst in from the kitchen, bowl in hand. Another woman called to her, across the room, "Are you having a date tonight?"

Between them lay a sea of Zendiks; maybe two-thirds of the Farm's sixty-plus members filled every chair, couch, and patch of rug. The lemon scent of Murphy's Oil fused with the glow of standing lamps to bathe us in resinous incandescence.

Forks clanged against stainless steel. Chatter rolled past me like delicate thunder.

The short woman nodded, her face erupting in a joyous grin. I felt a prick of envy. It must be so lovely, I thought, to go out for dinner and a movie with a guy you like, then return, in cricket-quiet, to this cozy old farmhouse. Never mind that none of the handful of dates *I'd* been on—all as a teenager in New York City—had involved dinner and a movie. This was

Polk County, North Carolina. The sticks. People here *must* mimic the mating behavior of characters in *Sweet Valley High* books and *Archie* comics. I wondered why the woman going on the date had gotten food for herself. Wouldn't she be eating out, with her boyfriend?

I took another bite of brown rice and pinto beans, topped with fresh salsa. I snapped off the sweet white stem of a leaf of romaine. I was eating the same food as the others. But the bowl I ate from, the fork I ate with, set me apart. They warned that Zendik warmed as you pushed toward the center. I was at the outer rim. I would have to earn my way in.

Minutes earlier, a graceful young woman named Eile had shown me to the shelves where bowls, plates, mugs, spoons, forks, and knives were stored. I was to pick one of each and mark it with my name, in felt-tip pen on masking tape. "You'll be on quarantine for ten days," she said, "which means you can't cook or wash dishes or eat from the same dishes we eat from."

"Okay," I said, feeling as though I'd just broken out in sores only I couldn't see. No commune I'd visited before Zendik had placed me on quarantine. Eile shrugged in apology. "It's just that we live so close to each other," she said. "If one of us comes down with a bug, everybody gets it."

I folded the rest of the romaine leaf into my mouth. Eile joined me on the floor. "So, how'd you find out about Zendik?" she asked.

"I saw it in *The Communities Directory.*" The *Directory* was an encyclopedia of well over a thousand groups, most in North America and devoted to homesteading. I'd ordered it the previous winter and pored over it in my Harvard dorm room. The next spring, just before graduation, I'd won a $13,500 travel grant to spend a year visiting some of these communities.

My grant proposal wasn't the first stage in a master plan. I had no master plan—only a couple tropisms: away from school and jobs, toward being outside and touching what was alive.

After eighteen years in classrooms, I yearned to put my *body* to work, as something more than a dolly for my brain. To learn sources of food, water, warmth, and shelter, beyond "the supermarket," "the tap," "the furnace," and "the landlord." I sought a story broader and sweatier than the one I'd grown up in. Touring villages rooted in the back-to-the-land movement seemed like a good start.

By the time I arrived at Zendik, on October 26, 1999, I'd stepped into a few communal stories, none strong enough to hold me for long. I'd spent three weeks at the Reevis Mountain School of Self-Reliance in the Superstition Mountains near Roosevelt, Arizona, where the ruling couple seemed pleased with their seclusion and the only other intern left before I did. A day and two nights at Alpha Farm in Deadwood, Oregon, where I was told to sit in the garden and give it my "love energy" (subtext: we're overwhelmed by our own chaos; we can't help you with yours). A night at the San Francisco Zen Center's Green Gulch Farm in Muir Beach, California, whose dense fog of patience made me wonder where people buried their snarls, their irritations, their hatreds—and where, if I lived there, I would bury mine. Back home in Brooklyn, I'd taken the ferry to Staten Island for Friday-night dinner at Ganas, where most of the men were pale or gray-haired and the aim of the full-group mealtime discussion—an example, I was told, of "feedback therapy"—seemed to be to elicit bewildered, angry tears from the two women at the center of the ring. Soon after that, I'd sold myself on visiting Zendik—using its *Directory* listing, its fledgling website, and a phone conversation with Zylem, the veteran Zendik in charge of recruiting. Then I'd boarded a Greyhound bus to Hendersonville, North Carolina. A couple of Zendiks had retrieved me from the depot after completing the Farm's weekly shopping. I was loosely planning on staying two weeks.

When I mentioned *The Communities Directory*, Eile's eyes

lit up. "Really?" she said. "Me too! But I think we're the only ones. Most people showed up because of the magazine."

I'd flipped through my first Zendik magazine earlier that evening, in the backseat of the car that had brought me to the Farm. I'd zeroed in on a story by a woman named Karma about a Zendik road trip to Woodstock's corporate reincarnation the previous summer.

"You guys go on road trips to hand out magazines, right? Like that trip you took to Woodstock?"

"Yeah," said Eile. "We go out most weekends. When the concert scene is slow, we sell the street."

I could tell that "sell the street" meant "sell merchandise on the street." What threw me was the word "sell." "So, you don't just hand the magazines out? You *sell* them?"

"Yeah, that's how we support ourselves. We get donations sometimes, and apprentice fees, but they're not reliable. Selling is our survival."

Selling for a living sounded intriguing—but I doubted I could do it. Once, I'd spent an afternoon distributing free copies of the *New York Observer* on a busy corner in SoHo. I'd crumpled under the neutral cruelty of brush-off after brush-off, while my partner, laughing and bantering, had rapidly emptied his satchel.

"Does everybody go selling?" I asked.

"No, not everyone. I mean, almost all the girls do, every other weekend. But some of the guys aren't that good at it, so they only go out once in a while."

As Eile spoke, I noticed a bright fringe of scarves, shirts, and sweaters trimming the rail of the loft above the living room. "What's up there?"

"That's where a bunch of the girls sleep. We just moved in a couple weeks ago. The guys don't mind the draft in the barn, but for us it was getting to be too cold at night."

Uphill from the Farmhouse, at the end of a wide gravel path, stood two barns—one for horses, one for goats. Before dinner, Eile had led me up the hill, pointing out studios for music and dance, a woodshop adjoining a trash shed, a storage yard for building materials salvaged from demolition jobs in nearby towns. Then I'd followed her up a steep, rail-less staircase to the horse-barn loft. A few dozen bunks lined the loft's long sides. Wind slipped in through gaps between wall slats. These bunks slept most of the Zendik men.

At the back of the loft stood an insulated plywood box, about eight feet tall and twice as wide. Half the ten bunks inside the box belonged to a motley crew of strange males who, like me, were "new people." These would be my roommates.

Sitting with Eile in the living room, admiring the gaily decked railing, I wished I didn't have to trek up to the barn in the dark. I wondered what would earn me a bed here, among women.

The next morning, after breakfast, I reported for my first Zendik work assignment: helping dig a trench for running power cables from the Farmhouse to the dance studio. I waited outside the dance-room door, at one end of the Day-Glo-orange line sprayed on the ground as a guide. The rest of the crew—all women—sauntered up a dirt path from the toolshed, shouldering half a dozen shovels and a pickax.

Karma was first to grab the pick. She straddled the line, knees bent, quads taut against tight jeans, and hoisted it above her head. With a fierce downswing, she drove it deep in the earth.

Her hair slipped from a loose knot and tumbled in blond hanks to her shoulders, veiling the iridescent dreamcatchers dangling from her ears. Her low-cut T-shirt, tie-dyed in sea colors, barely hid pert, braless breasts. She'd perfected the *macha*-yet-feminine look favored by Zendik women.

"Yeah!" she grunted, slipping her hand down the pick's shaft for a second swing. "Nothin' like a little pickin' to get the blood movin' in the mornin'!" The daughter of a Texas-based diplomat, she'd had ample opportunity to hone her hillbilly act.

When it was my turn to pick, my heartbeat accelerated with excitement. Blood rushed to my cheeks. Euphoria surged through me as dormant muscles roared into use.

"Yeah! Swing it!" yelled Karma. I glanced over my shoulder at her. Heaving a shovelful of clods over the lip of the trench, she flashed me a mischievous grin. I smiled back, then redoubled my attack on the line of glowing orange. Each thwack of the pick swelled a joy I'd rarely taken in my innate strength.

"Hey, Helen!" called Karma, from a few feet farther back. I swiveled to face her and rested the pick against the building, guessing my turn with it had ended. She stood with one foot in the ditch, the blade of her trenching shovel poised to slice into the gray muck beneath the red clay. She knitted her eyebrows and thrust her jaw into geezer jowls, mugging for me and a couple other women who'd paused to listen. "Are you a lez-bean?"

What? I thought. But I could see why she'd asked. My baggy brown overalls hid every curve her jeans exposed. The neckline of my shirt clung to my collarbone. I owned no jewelry. After years of disuse, my ear piercings had almost closed. And my head evoked a shag rug—four and a half months earlier, a couple hours after receiving my college diploma, I'd given myself a buzz cut. Knowing I'd be wandering, I'd wished to spare myself the bother of keeping my hair clean—while showing my disinterest in *doing anything* to attract a man.

According to the mating story I'd brought to Zendik, the man I was meant to spend my life with would find *me*. He would see through my butch do and bad clothes. He would know that when I blushed—when I shunned his gaze for a book, the floor, the distance—I was subtly showing interest. He would reach beneath my silence and hunch to stroke my soft animal, curled and panting. He would fold me in his arms, set me at ease, sweep me to ecstasy. He would call, I would respond. Out of his touch would spring a lifelong bond.

I'd already begun wondering if this man would find me at Zendik.

Earlier that morning, through half-closed lids, I'd watched as a Zendik named Estero let himself into the plywood box at the back of the barn loft. Starting with thick, red-faced Rebel, snoring from a bunk opposite me, Estero roused each of my roommates with a touch to the shoulder and a cry of "Seven thirty! Rise and shine!" He ranged through the room with slouching grace, his dark curls pulled carelessly into a tangled ponytail. A tiny smile played at the edges of his eyes and mouth. Maybe it amused him to alarm others while still groggy himself. I snuggled into my mummy bag, eyes shut tight, and feigned the steady breathing of deep sleep.

I felt the air shift as he crouched to reach me. I kept my eyes closed. Then—there it was: the touch on my shoulder, igniting a tingle through layers of nylon, goose down, cotton. I let my eyes open to meet Estero's eyes, dark and wide, lit by that hint of a smile. "Seven thirty. Time to wake up," he said.

"Okay," I said. "I'm awake."

I lay still, transfixed, as he rose like steam from a hot spring and disappeared through the door.

Later, at breakfast, I'd washed down my bowl of honey-drizzled oatmeal with an intoxicating drink from the Farm's brimming pool of rippling masculinity. Tucked in a corner of the living room, I'd sipped surreptitious glimpses of firm biceps browned by farmer tans, frayed cuffs over muddy work boots, roughened hands resting on comfortably slung tool belts. I'd savored the notes of a new music of male names: Dymion. Prophet. Lyrik. Estero. (Again: Es*t*ero.) With their lively eyes and vigorous strides, their ease with the work of survival, the Zendik men seemed like a breed apart from the scholars and artists I'd known at Harvard.

But Karma couldn't read my insides. And she wasn't the first to miscast me. A few months earlier, in the ladies' room of an Applebee's on Flatbush Avenue, a woman had snarled,

"What are *you* doing here?" before seeing I was female. Her mistake had stunned and hurt me.

"No," I told Karma, the word "lez-bean" still ringing in my inner ear. "No, I'm really not. I just cut my hair short so it would be easy to take care of."

"I get it," said Karma, dropping her hillbilly act. "I was just curious. We like to get things clear around here, you know? Lay it all out in the open!" With a friendly wink, she sliced her shovel deeper into the ditch. Gripping the pick again, I wondered if staying at Zendik would make me anywhere near as sexy as she was.

Later that morning, Toba, one of just a few older women on the Farm, recruited me to help her build a cinder-block furnace house for the Addition, a new, two-story building at the crest of a hill opposite the one I'd climbed the night before. The sun rose behind the Addition and set behind the barns, passing at midday over the Farmhouse.

Toba stopped by the Farmhouse porch to load two fifty-pound sacks of Portland cement into a rusted blue wheelbarrow. She grabbed its shafts, and I followed her up a dirt track, past a manufactured home on stilts—the Mobile. I'd heard it was overcrowded and that its residents would ascend to the much larger Addition once it was finished.

At the construction site, Toba dropped both sacks on a patch of mortar-stained grass, then slit one open and emptied it into the wheelbarrow. Behind her a chop saw whined through siding, sending off the burnt-sugar scent of fresh sawdust. Hammers rang against nail heads as a half-dozen men fixed planks to the building's last bare flank. I crimped and straightened the hose at Toba's command, watching her pull the mixing hoe through the moistening glop with swift, sure strokes. She was lean, slim, tanned, and at least as *macha* as the younger women on my trenching crew.

Her T-shirt's plunging V-neck revealed a deeply hollowed collarbone. Lips pressed into a thin line, she focused on her work.

With the mortar moist and smooth as cookie dough, Toba handed me a trowel and showed me how to lay it in twin tracks along the inner and outer edges of the top layer of cinder blocks. I asked how she'd wound up at Zendik.

Her journey had begun twenty years earlier, when she'd left Winnipeg—her hometown—to study psychology at Simon Fraser University in Vancouver. She'd abandoned academia in search of something better after ending her marriage to an aspiring professor.

"He was always in his head, you know?" she said, rounding the long "o" into a northern "awh." "*My* biggest problem is that I'm so shut down emotionally. I needed to be in a place where people would call me on my bullshit. Force me to get in touch with what's in *here*." She stabbed the point of her mortaring trowel toward her heart. "People just get so hard, they build so many walls, living in the Deathculture. You have to, to survive, you know? And then you can't let anybody in, not even the people who love you. I wouldn't even think of raising Eave out there." Toba had given birth to Eave, now three, at Zendik. She was one of the Farm's three children. "Deathculture," I knew from the Zendiks' magazine and website, was their term for the outside world, where competition and lying were killing everything: humans, animals, ecosystems, joy, love, friendship. I neither shared this view nor shied away from it. I had yet to firm a story of why we hurt each other and ourselves.

As we laid track and set blocks, Toba sped through the questions I'd answered a half-dozen times since arriving at Zendik: Where was I from, how had I heard about the Farm, how long was I planning to stay? Then she picked up the line of questioning Karma had started.

"Do you have a boyfriend?" she asked.

"No, I don't," I said, blood flooding my cheeks. Like her,

I'd come to Zendik untethered by romance. No man would tug me back home.

"Ay," she said, with a quick nod. "Have you ever had a boyfriend?"

"Yeah, once, in high school."

Toba nodded again, urging me on.

"We lasted about two months. He dumped me the day I called to say I'd gotten into Harvard. I asked him why, and he said we were too different. I was too eccentric."

I paused, recalling the helpless sobs of that breakup. I'd met the boy—Frank—by matching his pace in an undeclared footrace. I was a senior at Dominican Academy, a rigorous but modest Catholic girls' school on Manhattan's Upper East Side. He was a junior at Regis, the city's most prestigious school for Catholic boys. Each October, to raise funds, DA and Regis staged a joint walkathon. Almost all the girls and some of the boys strolled the ten- or twelve-mile route, immersed in flirtation and gossip. I, like many of the Regis guys, speed-walked. It didn't matter that there was no prize. We wanted to *win*.

Stopped short by a DON'T WALK sign on Central Park West, Frank introduced himself and I reciprocated. Later that day, back at Regis, we slipped out of the thronged courtyard to wander the school's cavernous halls. He described the calisthenic feats he'd need to perform to make the cut at West Point; I told him I'd applied early action to Harvard. It was then—before we'd even started dating—that he posed his condemning hypothetical: "So, if you got into Harvard but you were going out with a guy who couldn't do better than, say, some SUNY school, would you ditch Harvard for SUNY to be with him?"

"No way!" I said. If I heard the doom in his words, I dismissed it. Plenty of couples in books stayed in love long-distance.

"It was fitting that he called me eccentric, I guess," I told

Toba, "since 'eccentric' also means 'elliptical' and I have the same birthday as Johannes Kepler—the guy who discovered that the planets orbit in ellipses."

Kepler's predecessor Nicolas Copernicus had correctly posited that the planets orbit the sun—while perpetuating the fallacy that they move in circles. To cement his story against contradictory observations, he added dozens of circular suborbits. Sixty-odd years after Copernicus died, Kepler rolled out elliptical motion and cleared the suborbits away.

If Toba found my Kepler comment funny, or dorky, she didn't show it.

"So that was it, ay? You haven't done anything since?"

"Actually, I have," I said, flipping my trowel too quickly and dropping a glop of cement. Hardly anyone knew what I'd done since Frank. Within my family, I sensed—imagined? created?—a taboo on discussing sexual experience. I was too shy to mention my escapades to my girlfriends, and only one or two had ever drawn them out.

"I fooled around with a couple guys I met on the road. In Arizona and Key West."

I'd met JJ in March 1998, toward the end of a yearlong break between my junior and senior years at Harvard. Wandering the Sonoran desert south of Tucson, afraid my detour from school had been a mistake, I'd befriended a trio of locals at Arivaca Lake. One of them set me up with a place to stay. I'd be sleeping—by myself, he assured me—in his friend JJ's *extra* trailer.

JJ had other plans. That night, after treating me to dinner at the Feed Barn and taking me four-wheel driving to the local catfish pond, he brought me to the crest of FM Hill—so called because from here, a car radio could pick up the Tucson music stations. Through the windshield I glimpsed the shadowy hulk of the Santa Rita Mountains and the lights of Arivaca, sprinkled across the sleeping valley. I felt the chill caress of winter on the cusp of spring through the pickup's rolled-down windows; the nubbly weave of the dingy bench seat; and a callused hand, suddenly clutching my knee.

JJ had made his move, as I'd been hoping he would. My touch-starved skin tingled in gratitude. He leaned in to kiss me, his dank cigarette breath slithering up my nostrils, his coarse beard and mustache rasping my cheeks and chin. Back at his trailer, he came to bed scrubbed and nude under a bear-skin rug. I luxuriated in his sinuous heat and the wonder of being entirely unclothed with a man for the first time. Maybe *this* was what I'd been wandering toward. Maybe *this* was how I'd dissolve my doubts and settle into now.

But when JJ lifted his head from my crotch and slid his chest onto mine, cock hard, I shook my head. "I don't wanna have sex," I said. I wished to share my sexual initiation with a man who might be my mate—not a rough-spoken ranch hand who reckoned I could stick around, keep house for him, pick up a shift at the Feed Barn.

I pulled back from the brink of sex again in January 1999, under cover of night, at the tip of a dock snaking into the Gulf of Mexico. I was in Key West on winter break from college; my seducer was Jorge, a suave Chilean graduate student who'd come on to me by resting a warm hand on my back and tilting my eyes toward the belt of Orion. I thrilled to his touch—and ignored the e-mail he sent, a month later, saying he'd like to see me on a trip he was planning to Boston.

Had Toba asked, I would have shared details of my flings with JJ and Jorge. But she just nodded, eyes on the block she was setting. Then she looked up. "Did you make it with them?" she asked.

"'Make it'? What do you mean?" Some of the sixties-isms the Zendiks favored needed translation.

"Have sex," she said. "Did you have sex with them."

Blood rushed to my cheeks again. The thrill of being recognized as a sexual being overrode any alarm I might have felt at the trespass in her question.

"No," I replied. "Both guys were ready, but I stopped them. I didn't wanna get pregnant. And I didn't wanna do it for the first time with just anyone."

As I spoke, I flashed on Karma's description, in her Woodstock story, of approaching a bare-chested man with the magazine: "I liked the painter even though I had to shield against too strong of a sexual connection. . . . Sex in the world isn't friendly yet." Had I avoided sex "in the world" partly because I'd sensed it wasn't friendly? Could it be true that sex at Zendik *was* friendly already? In a scenelet of the selling crew's drive home from upstate New York to North Carolina, Karma quoted her fellow road warrior Cayta—"who's in charge, if anyone's in charge"—as saying, "I always want to have sex on the way home—clean bed, hot food, and sex." Maybe, at the Farm, sex was something warm and sweet and easy to come by that you enjoyed with the blessing of friends. Maybe choosing the right matrix mattered just as much as meeting the right man.

My task after lunch was to help Zeta—one of the young women from the trenching crew—paint shelving units on the Addition's upper level, divided into three bedrooms. The one we set up in was a loft at the crest of a spiral staircase, bright with sunshine pouring in through windows and skylights. From the railing I admired the structure's soaring floor-to-roof sweep, as well as the love glowing through each handcrafted detail. I would not have guessed that every board in the building had been pried from the skeleton of some rotting home or shop. The Zendiks had taken a motley jumble of derelict stuff and found purpose for it in a smooth new whole.

Zeta filled two yogurt containers with thick white paint from a bucket nested in newspaper. As we laid it in sleek glides over rough reclaimed pine, I learned that she, like me, had grown up in New York City. She'd even attended the same high school as my sister, at about the same time. A musical virtuoso, she played violin and sometimes sang backup in the all-improv Zendik band. She met her *machisma* quotient with high-topped combat boots, and tiny-toothed shells biting into her dreadlocks. At the Farm about a year and a half, she was one of only two Black women in the group, and one of only three Black Zendiks.

Warmed by news of our shared origins, I barely blinked when Zeta switched subjects. "Hey," she said, with a playful smile, "has anyone told you how dating works?"

"No," I said. "But last night at dinner I heard one of the girls say she was going on a date. I figured she and her boyfriend were heading into Hendersonville to see a movie or something."

Watching Zeta's smile widen, I began to doubt the story I'd supplied. "Was I wrong?"

Zeta laughed and nodded, eliciting a burst of clicks from the tiny teeth. "Yeah, you were wrong," she said. "Dating here is nothing like dating out there. The way we do it is totally different." She paused, raised her brush to remove a stray bristle. "Have you met Shure and Loria?"

I hadn't.

"They're the dating strators. They've been here forever—I think since Boulevard."

"Strator," I would discover, was Zendik slang for "administrator." Boulevard—a town outside San Diego—was one of the Farm's earlier locations. Other Zendik vintages, from older to newer, included Topanga, Texas, and Florida. In its thirty-year history, the Farm had moved many times.

I nodded. Zeta continued. "If you wanna get together with a guy you like, you ask one of them to hit him up for you. You can hit him up for a date—which means sex—or if you just wanna kiss, hold hands, make out, you can start with a walk instead."

My brush slowed as I imagined ambling through a meadow at midnight, hand in hand, with Estero. The thought of my fingers twined in his roused a delicious wave of tingles.

"You can say in advance how far you wanna go, and the guy will respect that. No games, no pressure. No dumb pickup lines."

My vision dissolved into the final scene of a vivid dream I'd had when I was ten. A handsome man, at least thrice my age, was chasing me through a tropical forest. Upon catching me, he said, "Let's not have sex. Let's just make love." I was relieved and enraptured.

Twelve years later, I still thought "making love" and "having sex" were separate things. To me, "making love" meant luxuriating in the holding and kissing, the stroking and petting, the languor and longing, as long as you chose. This, it seemed, was the promise of a "walk."

Zeta broke in with a question. "You're a virgin, right?"

"Yeah," I said, taken aback. "How'd you know?"

"Oh," she said, dabbing extra paint into a knothole, "Toba told me. At lunch." She covered the patch around the knothole with short, quick strokes. "So, yeah, you'd wanna take it slow. Here, you can do that. People will help."

I thought again of Estero—the latest in a string of crushes threading back to first grade. How many boys, then men, had enthralled me with their wit, their salt, their sweat, only to dance out of reach? How many chances had I missed to take a hand, test for a match?

Where had Zendik been all my life?

"Wow," I breathed, gazing out the bedroom window at a pillow of mist falling on the Blue Ridge. "That sounds like a fairy tale."

A couple days later, I caught my first glimpse of Arol, the Farm's matriarch. Glancing up from my lunch bowl of salad and broiled tofu, I saw a silver-haired woman sitting opposite me, in an arm-chair by the door to the porch. At sixty-one, Arol was a generation or two older than the rest of the Zendik women, who ranged in age from late teens to early forties.

She looked older in person than she did in pictures. On the cover of *We the Poet*, the Zendik band's latest album, her hair fell in shining ripples; her skin, smooth and youthful, luminesced behind a wall of rain. In a Zendik magazine photo taken about ten years earlier, she commanded a barn door-way, hip thrust out, slim and sexy in jeans, cowboy boots, and a tailored denim jacket. Her luxuriant hair spilled over her shoulders in dark waves tinged gray; the dime-size blue whale tattooed high on her right cheekbone faced a rocky voyage past the challenge hurled by her stormy gaze: *I dare you to say I'm on the fade.*

Since she'd posed for the photo, Arol had overseen two moves (from Texas to Florida and then North Carolina), lost Wulf, her mate of forty years, and aged in frame and face. The woman across the living room wore a baggy sweater and loose cotton pants. Gravity tugged at her cheeks, her neck, the dime-size whale; wrinkles webbed her forehead. Her hair, still thick around her shoulders but brittle at the ends, had faded to gray.

My mother, a month shy of fifty-seven, had been pinning her hair back in a neat bun for as long as I could remember and teaching Catholic school for nearly twenty years. She pre-ferred the wings to the spotlight. Yet it was my trust in her that primed me to trust Arol. Had Wulf been alive and giving orders, I might have fled the Farm within days.

Arol was murmuring what seemed like instructions to a flint-chipped man crouched at her elbow. A dark, billed cap obscured his eyes. He nodded every few seconds. Her lips almost grazed his ear. This was Prophet, Arol's consort. He was a year older than I, and just six months older than Swan, Arol and Wulf's daughter. They'd gotten together a few months after Wulf's death.

When Arol finished, Prophet nodded once more and gently squeezed her forearm. He rose to leave the room, never raising his gaze to reveal his eyes. Cap brim, nose, mustache, goatee—a study, in living quartz, of precision focus. The room filled with the clatter and click of fork against bowl, fork against plate. Arol looked up. At me.

"You're Helen, right? The Harvard chick. Where'd you come here from?"

"New York City. Brooklyn."

"Ha! That's where *I* grew up. The projects. Williamsburg, Hell's Kitchen." She laughed. "New York's a real shithole, isn't it?"

I smiled at her bluntness. I, too, loathed New York, in moments, for its crowds and concrete, its everyday brutality; I welcomed the idea that it didn't suit humans. If that was true, then I was right to bail out. On the other hand, it was home, the place I knew best. I'd long thought that if there were a foot-race up Broadway, complete with real-life rush-hour throngs, ill-timed DON'T WALK signs, and motor vehicles threatening pedestrians in the crosswalk, I'd win. I was that skilled at the dance of the city. And I'd been lucky enough to grow up in a large apartment on Prospect Park West—affordable for a family on food stamps because we'd moved to Brooklyn in 1977, when the South Slope was rowdy and rents were low. I tried for a compromise between contradicting Arol and unduly dissing my roots.

"Well, yeah, it can get pretty ugly. But I didn't mind living there when I was a kid."

Arol lifted one corner of her mouth in a sardonic smile, then switched subjects. "You know, we work pretty hard here. It's not like college. It's a much deeper commitment. You have to be smart to make it, but that's not all. You have to put your *heart* in it. You think you can do that?"

She stared at me, her eyes storming mine. I wasn't sure what she meant, but *she* seemed to know, and I was intrigued by the story taking form: At Zendik I'd grow in new ways, working toward rewards at once more real and mysterious than grants and grades. Revive sweetness in romance. Practice the mating dance without leaving home.

chapter 2

Moving In

I'D JUST PULLED ON MY shirt and underpants, and was stepping into my overalls, when I heard a knock on the door to
the Farmhouse bathroom. Thinking the knocker was next in
the shower line snaking through the living room, I opened my
mouth to say, "I'll be right out!" But before I could speak, the
knob turned. My heart lurched. The door swung open, and
Cayta strode in. I stepped back into a patch of morning sunshine and yanked my pants up to my waist.

In her Woodstock story, Karma had said that Cayta was
in charge, if anyone was—and she looked it now, the corners of
her mouth drawn down in half-moon grooves. Though she was
seven days my junior, her five years at Zendik made her seem
older and wiser than I was. She reminded me of Miss Clavel,
the spinster headmistress in the *Madeline* children's book who
marched her "twelve little girls" in "two straight lines." Except
that Cayta—like most of the Zendik women—glowed with
youth and health. Freckles sprinkled her creamy skin. From a
deep widow's peak, her thick, dark locks flowed into a single,

smooth braid. Woven to a vanishing point, the braid, though unbound, stayed fast.

Cayta looked at me and shook her head. "Helen, you're a dirty girl," she said.

I tugged the bib of my overalls up over my shirt and fastened the straps. The trickle of resistance raised by Cayta's invasion disappeared in a flush of shame. She was right. For the past week, I'd been turning compost, shoveling goat muck, denailing boards, prying siding off a derelict house in a nearby town. In the three or four days I'd been allowing between showers, grime shadows had crept up my calves and around my neck. But bathing was a challenge. All forty-plus of us bunking in the barn and Farmhouse were expected to be on call for work crews from breakfast till dinner—which translated into morning and evening rushes on the one shower we all shared. Under these circumstances, bathing twice a week seemed reasonable. *I* didn't mind, and it hadn't occurred to me that the Zendiks might. Hadn't the website warned visitors to bring work boots and clothes that could get dirty, since these were "pioneer times"? Wasn't I—weren't many of us—living in a barn?

"Yeah, I know," I said, studying a swirl of white flecks in the viridian linoleum. "But the shower line is always so long, and—"

Cayta cut me off. "If you wanna stay here, you're gonna have to get used to sharing a hell of a lot more than you did out there." I thought to defend myself: *But I don't* mind *sharing. I'm* happy *to let other people use the shower, instead of me.* Before I could speak, Cayta continued: "There are a bunch of us. We live close to each other. It's not like out in the world, where everyone has their own house, their own car, their own everything."

She softened her salvo with a half smile and leaned back against the toilet tank, folding her hands in her lap. Her fingernails, I noted, were filed into ovals—and clean. They were *clean.* Cayta lived in the Mobile. "Seems like you have a pretty strong body odor," she said.

The flush of shame returned, deeper this time. Dirt layered my surface; scent seeped from within. What other betrayals lurked beneath my skin?

"Yeah, I guess so." I reached for my deodorant.

She wrinkled her nose and sniffed. "What kind of deodorant *is* that?"

"Mint julep. Queen Helene." I held the stick out to her—riddled with chemicals, jungle green. I hadn't used another brand in years.

"That stuff is *stinky,*" she said. "Y'know, you can use the communal deodorant."

She pointed to a Tom's of Maine regiment on a spruce-green shelf: neat rows of evergreen (for men) and unscented (unisex). Above the deodorant stood two wide-mouthed mason jars jammed with mongrel packs of toothbrushes, bristles gnawed and ragged.

"Yeah, other people have noticed your odor, too," she warned, as she rose from the toilet and made for the door. "Even the guys. So you need to work on that, okay?"

"Okay." *Which guys? Is one of them Estero?*

Alone again, I extracted my toothbrush from one of the packs and squeezed out a gob of chalky tan paste, tasting of clay and licorice. In the mirror as I brushed, I saw a shaggy-headed woman with an anxious gaze. "Don't worry, Helen," I began—before recalling that someone sitting near the door in the living room might be listening. *You're gonna be okay. Sometimes you have to change a few things to make it in a new place.*

The next morning, I reached the Farmhouse early enough to avoid the shower line. Once clean, I repaired to the living room to read while I waited for breakfast. From a stack of Zendik magazines in the bottom drawer of a scratched filing cabinet, I chose an issue published a year earlier. I skipped over the Zendik philosophy and stopped at a personal essay by Kro, the only Black man at the Farm.

The essay begins, "It is a Friday night like any other and I am drunk, horny and 17 years old." At seventeen, Kro leads a double life: by day he's "senior class Most Studious, three-time Student Council member, Youth Advisor to the local Congressman"; by night, he's "a hormone-crazed, clueless cruiser of parties, searching for something sane, something sweet, some reason to live my life."

After one such party, he finds himself giving a ride to a floppy-drunk fifteen-year-old girl in a short skirt. When she, for no apparent reason, "suddenly sits up and turns around, raises herself up onto her knees and leans over the tilted front seat," he reaches over and grasps her leg, then inches his hand up to her crotch and under her panties. Not even sure she's conscious, he recoils when she makes a slight shift. That's when the guilt and shame set in, "the unending refrain . . . What am I doing? What have I done?"

Kro had kept his trespass secret for more than a decade by the time he drafted the story and read it aloud to his "friends here at the Farm" at lunch one day. He implied that their empathy had helped him shed the spiritual analogue of "a leech fastened to tender flesh" and revise his view of his actions: "I was really just a sweet child, caught in a cultural vortex of ignorance and diminished expectations . . . designed to get your head spinning so badly that you'll settle for anything—date rape, molestation, or just your basic, sloppy, drunken fuck and tumble." His ideal was "a culture where sex is accepted as the benevolent pulse of pleasure . . . a culture where no one—no one—has to give up her wasted body to a stranger in order to obey the stirrings of sexual love." He lived at Zendik Farm, he said, because "there's no other way for me—or anyone else—to ever feel the awesome beauty of clean, sweet Love." Here was a variation on Karma's lament that "sex in the world isn't friendly yet."

Kro's tale gripped me with its precision and honesty. I was there in the driver's seat, quick with the thrill of transgressing, there in the passenger seat, stilled by near oblivion. But when play-by-play gave way to interpretation, the story line turned at once too blurry and too sharp.

What—I wonder now—had happened to transmute a repentant sexual predator into a "sweet child," blameless in the whirl of "a cultural vortex"? Why did Kro imply that his passed-out victim had complied in her own violation—that she, too, had been "obey[ing] the stirrings of sexual love"? How did he know that no one beyond Zendik had ever felt, or would ever feel, "the awesome beauty of clean, sweet Love"?

After I'd flipped to a different story, the door from the porch groaned open and Kro trudged in, looking sleepy and grumpy. He was in charge of starting and tending the fire that burned in the woodstove throughout the day and into the night. Once he'd crumpled newspaper for tinder and coaxed a flame from the kindling, I wished him good morning. I had questions for him—not about his essay, but about East Wind, where he'd lived for three years. I'd considered going there instead of Zendik.

East Wind, a twenty-five-year-old charter member of the Federation of Egalitarian Communities, lay cradled in the Ozark foothills a few miles from Tecumseh, Missouri. The same day Zylem had told me I was welcome to visit Zendik, I'd received an invitation—handwritten, adorned with stars and butterflies, signed "Twilight"—to participate in East Wind's upcoming three-week visitor period. Visitors worked a set number of hours per week—gardening, cooking, cleaning, weaving rope sandals, grinding nuts into butter. After three weeks, they became eligible for provisional membership; six months later, they could apply to be full members.

After reading Twilight's note, I weighed the sheet of loose-leaf in my hand against the phone conversation I'd just had with

Zylem. East Wind's offer was defined, time-bound, something I could touch; Zendik's was ethereal, open-ended, an echo of a man's voice saying, "We don't have set work hours; we all pitch in to do what needs to get done." Saying, "Some people stay a couple weeks; some decide this is where they belong and stay for life." Saying, "We're not an *intentional community*—we're a new culture." The gaps he'd refused to fill with facts, I filled with fantasy: I saw comely, weathered young women—long hair flying, peasant skirts flaring—whirling in dance with ember-lit, rugged young men. They reveled in a rough barn, open on one side to a night sky misty and rainy, dark with no stars. I laid a veil of romantic longing over this tribe I'd never met, on this farm I'd never seen. While I appreciated East Wind's warmth and clear guidelines, I found my vision of Zendik far more enticing.

Having chosen Zendik, I was wondering what I'd miss if I stayed and *didn't* visit the other groups on my short list.

I waited for Kro to rise from his crouch in front of the stove door. "I heard you lived at East Wind for a few years. How'd you like it there?"

He grabbed a chunk of oak from a stack beside the stove and tossed it on the fire. "East Wind," he snorted. "Escapist hippie bullshit. It's just a hideout for a bunch of babies who won't face themselves. Sure, they live together and compost their shit. But they don't get straight. They take another drink, another hit."

Kro's indictment surprised me. (Maybe it wouldn't have if I'd spent more time with his essay—if I'd paused on the clause "there's no way for me—or anyone else.") Hadn't Zendik and East Wind both sprung from the sixties impulse to drop back to Earth and rebuild the village? Didn't Zendik at least owe East Wind a comrade's respect?

But maybe Kro was right. Maybe East Wind—along with Twin Oaks, Acorn, Sandhill, Dancing Rabbit—was just a crash pad for the average misfit. Hadn't I applied early action to Harvard and only Harvard, sure I'd get in and sure I belonged? Maybe I'd already found the elite advance guard of the commune movement. Maybe I didn't need to bother vetting other options.

"Oh," I said. Then, for lack of a better response, "So I guess you don't recommend visiting."

Kro scowled as he chucked another oak chunk into the stove, then banged the door shut. "Do what you want," he said. "I'm just saying, if you wanna be with people who are actually trying to change the way they relate to each other, you're not gonna find them at your average back-to-the-land 'egalitarian community.'"

I didn't ask Kro about Twin Oaks, the Virginia commune where he'd spent his second hiatus from Zendik. I didn't ask why he'd fled—twice—the one place where he thought love was possible.

Cayta strode into the living room and dropped onto the couch across from me. Dinner was over; the shower line had petered out; those going on "walks" and "dates" had gone on them. I was paging through another Zendik magazine. I had nothing else to read—I'd brought a journal but no books with me; the Zendiks had yet to unpack their library—and I didn't want to return to the plywood box in the barn loft, which felt to me like a ghetto. I looked up. She lasered me with her gaze. "You have to figure out why you hate men," she said. "Rebel says you're not social with him or the other guys *at all*—you dive into your mummy bag the moment you get back to your room, and then you get the hell out first thing in the morning. No wonder you've never had a serious boyfriend. You're gonna have to get to work on yourself if you want that to change."

Charge: you hate men. Evidence: you avoid your roommates; you've failed to sustain a romantic relationship. Verdict: guilty. Sentence: Find the roots of your faults. Rip them out. Revise yourself.

When your prosecutor doubles as judge, you have two choices: step into her sentence, or step out of the court and the story that supports it. The story, for all its rude twists, was growing only more fascinating. So I took the feeling "hate" and the group "men" and sought examples in my past of having joined them.

I didn't have to look far. I'd written my college application essay about why I hated my father and was glad my mother had divorced him. In high school—after being sexually assaulted in a New York City subway station by a man claiming to have a gun—I'd composed a sequel to Sophocles' *Antigone* in which Antigone's sister, Ismene, avenges her by storming Thebes with an army of Amazon warriors and putting Creon to death.

Also, I had an interest in serving Cayta's sentence. Like Zeta's disclosure of how dating worked, it hinted that I could *act* in search of lasting love. What kind of "work" on myself was she prescribing?

"You should do some writing," she said. "Start with your dad, your relationship with him. What went wrong there? Then your high school boyfriend, any other guys you liked. Write about how you are with guys now, how you treat them, how you act when you're around them. Write about sex—how you think it'll be, what *good* sex might feel like." She paused, pressing her palms into her knees for emphasis. "You have to get down to what your *philosophy* is, what you *believe* about men. Then you can get somewhere. Then you can change."

Listening to Cayta, I felt my past come alive, like pond scum under a microscope. What creatures—patterns, clues—pulsed within that seeming calm?

"Oh, and there's something else you might wanna write about with all that," she said.

"Yeah? What?"

"Psychic cause and effect."

I wrinkled my eyebrows. I'd skimmed over the term in the Zendik magazine without grasping its meaning.

Cayta pulled her braid over her shoulder and coiled its tip around her finger. "You know how Wulf says, 'You attract to yourself what you are'?"

I nodded. Though I couldn't place them, the words seemed familiar.

"That means you're always broadcasting your true desires out into the universe. Maybe you're unaware of what you want or why you want it. But you can bet that whatever you get is *your* cosmic pizza; it's exactly what *you* ordered."

I nodded again. I'd encountered similar ideas in Neale Donald Walsch's new age blockbuster, *Conversations with God*. According to Walsch—according to God?—the course of each human life is set by her soul's choices about what to experience during this round on Earth. Why would a soul ever choose pain, poverty, hate, violence over pleasure, wealth, love, peace? Because, said Walsch/God, souls have all the time in the world to explore the full range of human action and emotion, in quest of ever greater understanding.

Cayta continued, "That's the law of psychic cause and effect. That's how the universe works. So when you write out what you've been through with men, make sure you look at how you drew that stuff to you. Why you *wanted* it."

I didn't see any harm in flirting with this law. Why *not* give it a whirl on my mental dance floor? If it squeezed my ribs, I'd let it go. But what if it held true? What if I'd just been initiated into a revolutionary explanation—known only to an elite few—for *why things happen as they do*?

Later that night, hunched over my journal in my bunk, I went hunting for what had made me hate men. First I tagged my father's surly isolationism; my mother's fury with him; Frank's rejection; my perception of men as live grenades, to be approached with caution lest I provoke an explosion. Then I slowed to stalk the big game: the three sexual assaults I'd suffered as a fourteen-year-old commuting by subway to and from high school. Though I'd told this story before, I'd yet to write it down. Maybe, like Kro, I hoped to subdue a still-thrashing monster by fixing its details in print.

The first time: I was clutching a pole on a jam-packed downtown 6 train, shoulders aching under the straps of my knapsack. The doors closed at Fifty-Ninth Street. The thunder of steel rail against iron underbelly drowned out any warning rustle as the man to my rear crushed against me and snaked his fingers under my skirt. I stiffened. I didn't snarl. I didn't whirl on him, livid, and demand, "Just what the fuck do you think you're doing, asshole?" (I didn't utter the word "fuck" till I turned eighteen and my uncle urged me to try it. "You shouldn't be scared of a *word*," he said.) I thought, *If I move, someone will see.* His fingers slithered closer to my vagina. I held my breath. The longer the moment stretched, the more trapped I felt by that first beat of what seemed like acquiescence. *If I move, someone will see.*

As the train pulled into Fifty-First Street—my stop—the pack shifted. A gap opened. Someone saw. An older woman in a bulky, calf-length coat pounced on me with her gaze. "Don't let him rub up on you like that!" she said. I slunk through the doors to the piss-stained platform.

The second time: I was ascending an escalator between the downtown 6 stop at Fifty-First Street and the Brooklyn-bound F platform at Fifty-Third Street/Lexington Avenue. I felt the snap of leather against my calf. I kept my eyes fixed on the top step. The snap came again, with more sting. I glanced over my shoulder. A pockmarked boy a couple steps down was clutching something—a belt?—close to his thigh. I looked ahead again. A third snap. Then—the breached kilt, the slithering hand. The instinctive paralysis. A thought: *Should I kick him? No, that's unchristian. Turn the other cheek.*

At the crest of the escalator, the boy withdrew and walked off, smirking at the two boys traveling with him. They smirked back. Maybe he'd groped me on a dare.

The third time: I'd started taking the Q to the Upper East Side, to avoid both the 6 train and the Fifty-First/Fifty-Third Street transfer. The station at Sixty-Third and Lexington is one of the deepest in the New York City subway system. From the Queens-bound platform, you must climb one hundred vertical feet to reach sunlight.

I knew about boarding the train at the right spot. I knew that if I rode at the Q's head, it would disgorge me a few steps from the zigzag of stairs and escalators rising to street level. But that morning, dashing to a waiting Q from an arriving F, I'd wound up at the train's tail.

I was alone when I gained the vast landing at the top of the first stair.

Alone except for a man in a dark coat—padded, large pockets. A coat for shoplifting groceries or curling up on a cardboard sheet in a dark doorway. Above the collar: ratty dreadlocks, scruffy beard, bloodshot eyes. Below the hem: fraying cuffs over rotting loafers, shuffling toward me on grime-shadowed tile.

The man, forcing me to the wall with his fierce grip and thick stench. A front-pocket bulge, likely a poking finger but enough to still me when he said, "I have a gun. Don't move and don't scream, or I'll shoot you." Then: Hand up my skirt. Tongue prying my lips. Gust of old breath. Tongue on my tongue. Fingers in my underpants, up my vagina. A reaction harking back to every bare-bottom spanking I'd ever received over my father's knee: I peed. Piss wet my underpants and thighs, trickled down my socks to my shoes. Resistance? Or just terror, turned loose?

Then—shift. A fist broke in. A fist with a ring on it. A ring set with a large, hard stone. Fist, ring, stone. The man's head jerked to the side. He stumbled back. He flung a handful of change at me and fled down the steps to the train. The coins clattered to the floor.

The man whose fist it was gave me his card—he'd act as a witness, he said, if I wished to press charges. I raced up the stairs to the token booth. Choking out words through sobs, I told the clerk I'd been assaulted. Behind me, commuters churned through turnstiles. One paused, listened in, slapped me with a scolding: "What were you doing, riding at the wrong end of the train?"

Later, two detectives came to my school to record my complaint. The principal, sitting with me during the interview, vouched for my gentleness. "Helen wouldn't hurt a fly," she said.

This, I was beginning to understand, was a problem. Yes, in the thick of each attack, fear and shame had kept me still and silent. But there was something else: I had no story at the ready showing I could fight.

Soon after the third assault, I signed up for karate classes at an all-female dojo a half mile from home. There I learned to kick, punch, block, and *kiai*—yell—as I did so. A few months later, I wrote a short story in which a teenage girl, exiting a deserted subway station, fends off a band of young male predators with her kick and her *kiai* and ascends untouched to the sunlight. Thus I prepared myself: the next time a man laid a hand on me, I would fight.

My story did not prepare me to answer, or even recognize, subtler forms of attack. And so, in my bunk in the barn loft, after recording the details of the three assaults, I turned to the last part of Cayta's assignment: recasting my sexual history in terms of psychic cause and effect.

Having admitted that most of my sexual fantasies involved the man taking the lead—taking "advantage" of me—I sprouted an idea Cayta had seeded: "although none of [the assaults] was pleasurable—the third truly *was* terrifying and mind-numbing—

maybe my lack of response was not absolute, petrifying fear." In other words: maybe I'd *wanted* that hated touch.

A couple nights later, I took my journal to the living room to show Cayta. Sitting next to me on the couch nearest the woodstove, she read the three columns of neat black print as the embers crackled and hissed. I wondered if she'd praise me for my honesty. If she'd spot hidden patterns. My chest tingled with the thrill—and risk—of sharing secrets.

Cayta reached the bottom of the last column and turned the page to make sure she'd seen everything. Palm resting on the passage revising my take on why I hadn't fought, she turned to face me, a shrewd glint in her dark eyes.

"You were raised Catholic, right?"

"Yes," I said. This was common knowledge. My stock response to Zendiks' questions about my religious background was, "I'm a recovering Catholic."

She made a fist and pressed it against the blocks of text. "Don't you think you drew those assaults to you, since it was the only way you could have a sexual experience without feeling guilty?"

The tingle stilled. Maybe she was right—and this was a precious insight—but it hit me with a condemning thud.

"Well, maybe," I said.

"So, if you start going after sex on your own terms, you'll stop vibing into that shit." Cayta smiled. "That's pretty cool! And here you can do that."

I flashed on the Zendik dating scheme, its tantalizing possibilities. Could it really encase me in a shield of consensual touch? If so, then—maybe—*this was the place.*

My plan, when I'd boarded the bus to North Carolina in late October, had been to give Zendik two weeks. If I didn't like it, I'd hitchhike fifty miles west, through squat peaks and deep gaps, to the Appalachian Trail. I'd pick it up just east of the Tennessee border and march south toward Georgia.

By the second week in November, the wild persimmon trees at the top of the driveway were shedding their leaves. Each day, fewer fruits hit the ground in sweet vermillion goosplats. At night, a chill seeped through the seams in the plywood box's fur of pink fiberglass. Striking out for Georgia was swiftly losing appeal.

Scrunched inside my mummy bag one evening, only my eyes exposed, I caught hold of a question that always seemed to dart away from me in the bustle of the day: *Will I stay?*

Peering into the future, I glimpsed daunting decisions. My income tax return—which the grant would oblige me to file for the first time—was due in April. Complying, in my view, meant shoving meat down the maw of the US war monster. I'd long admired Dorothy Day and the Catholic Workers, who resisted war taxes by living in openhanded poverty, caring for anyone who showed up at a House of Hospitality. Back in late summer, I'd stopped into an IRS office to ask whether I'd still need to pay tax on the grant money if I gave it to charity. The answer was no. Surrendering my $300 apprentice fee to the Zendiks, shortly after learning how dating worked, I'd been glad to pass part of my windfall on to what seemed like a worthy cause.

More pressing than taxes were my $16,500 in student loans—part of the hefty financial aid package that had allowed me to attend a school whose yearly tuition rivaled my family's annual income. The loans would enter repayment and begin accruing interest on New Year's Day. I'd owe about $100 per month for the first five years, then about $250 per month for the next ten. I hadn't been thinking about how I'd pay the money back when I'd signed my first promissory note, on autopilot, at seventeen. During college, I'd dispelled debt-induced anxiety with the failsafe of bankruptcy—still an option until Congress nixed it in 1998. Yes, going bankrupt would have ruined my credit. But the threat seemed abstract, in a family where no one owned a house or a car or used a credit card.

Five months after graduation, I faced not just debt but expectation: that I would get a job with a regular paycheck and send a chunk of that paycheck to the Department of Education's Direct Loan Processing Center every month till I was thirty-eight. That I would embrace this arrangement out of gratitude for the nice salaries and professional opportunities made possible by my degree from Harvard. I hadn't known, at seventeen, that I was signing up for selective service in the extractive economy, or that five years later I'd be handed a draft card.

No, thank you, I thought, squeezing my eyes shut. Since entering preschool at the age of three, I'd been hewing to a preset storyline. I was ready—wasn't I?—to start my own story.

In a journal entry dated "Halloween," I'd written, "Idea: give all my money to Zendik, so the government can't get it. Write a letter to the Department of Education saying, *this* is my contribution to the education of the children of the future." The Zendik Farm Arts Foundation was registered with the IRS as a 501(c)(3) organization devoted to teaching "farm and life work skills in animal husbandry, horticulture, and trades including carpentry, mechanics, publishing, and music, arts, and crafts." Recurring two weeks into my immersion in Zendik culture, the idea seemed less a lark than it had at first. Plus, I'd known since I was a kid what a thrill it could be to give money away. In fourth grade, during Lent, I'd stuffed every cent I had into the cardboard "poor box" each student at my Catholic elementary school received from a missionary group called the Propagation of the Faith. I didn't know what the money would do for the suffering children depicted on the box; I didn't even know what

"Propagation" meant. I just knew I felt cleansed and reckless, exhilarated by a shift *I'd* chosen to make. In high school, when a wealthy friend of my mother's slipped me a $100 bill to cover a $17 cab ride home to Brooklyn from the Upper East Side, I handed the hundred to the driver and told him to keep the change. In college, on occasion, I gave $20 bills to spare-changers. My joy was complete in the moment of giving, which felt more like communion than receiving the host at Mass ever had.

Owen, the newest of the new guys, was up reading in the bunk across from mine. I scrunched deeper into my mummy bag, covering even my eyes now, to conserve body heat and block out his flashlight. I longed to be snug among women, in a bunk in the Farmhouse, the heat of Kro's fire rising through the floorboards. Maybe a big donation would smooth my path toward the Farm's heart.

I woke the next morning to a wave of doubt. *What? Give the Zendiks all my money? Am I crazy? Shouldn't I at least try a few other places before I commit?* I rolled onto my back and studied a mark on the underside of the top bunk. Was it shaped like a flame or an eye? *Maybe it would be good to go somewhere else—but then I'd have to go through the rigmarole of showing up and easing in all over again. And what if Zendik really is building a new culture? The way they do dating sure seems different.* I decided the mark could be either a flame *or* an eye, depending on what you thought of when you looked at it. *Maybe this is my chance to be part of something amazing. Maybe I'd be crazy* not *to give everything.*

At breakfast (scrambled eggs and short-grain brown rice in a bowl with no label, now that I'd served my ten-day quarantine), I told Teal—the woman who'd taken my apprentice fee—that I wanted to give the Farm my grant money. I'd already told her and other Zendiks how much I'd received and how little I'd spent. After paying the $300, I had thirteen thousand left.

Teal blinked, then nodded. "Okay, I'll tell Rayel. She's the one who usually handles that stuff." I'd met Rayel, but that was it. We hadn't worked together or conversed. She rarely ate at the Farmhouse.

I was shelving plates for lunch cleanup, my back to the kitchen's rear entrance, when I caught a whiff of rose oil, then the whoosh of the screen door closing and the click of cowboy boots against wood worn smooth. Rayel appeared at my side. Several inches shorter than I, she had to lift her chin to meet my eyes. But her straight spine and calm gaze made it clear who was in charge. "Helen," she said, "I hear you have money you wanna give us."

"I do."

"Are you sure? I wouldn't want you to do something you might regret."

I'd yet to discover that Rayel, who'd moved to Zendik at eighteen from a plush midwestern suburb, had funneled large sums from her family to the Farm—most notably, an investment in the land.

Back in 1987, indifferent to college but disturbed by humans' shaky perch on Earth, Rayel had told her parents that what she really wanted was to grow organic food. A newspaper ad her mother found led her to a homestead in the high desert near San Diego where young people could learn to farm. After Zendik relocated to a two-hundred-acre ranch outside Austin, she persuaded her dad to put up the funds for an adjoining hundred acres. He insisted the deed be in her name; maybe one day she and her mate would build a home and start a family on their own patch of riparian savanna. When Zendik moved again, first to Florida and then to North Carolina, Rayel's ownership carried over. Upon my arrival in 1999, she owned a half interest in the Farm's 116 acres. Years later, under duress, she would sign that interest over to Arol. Later still, she would regret it.

"Yes, I'm sure," I said, the thrill of giving swelling within me as a wide smile lit her eyes. "I wanna stay here. And I want you guys to have the money."

"Great!" she said. "Talk about perfect timing!"

On our walk up the hill to the Mobile, Rayel confided that the Farm was in a cash crunch caused by a delay in payment on the Florida property. I felt privileged to catch this glimpse of Zendik's inner workings; I doubted any of my roommates had ever come this close.

At the Mobile, Rayel had me wait on the porch while she slipped inside to get the phone. I tuned to the murmur behind the blinds but couldn't make out words. When she returned, I recited my information to a teller at Independence Savings Bank (soon to be gobbled by Sovereign Bank, which would in turn be chomped by financial giant Santander). Then Rayel took the receiver to complete the transfer, her tone calm and warm. With that, I joined the ranks of those who'd surrendered wealth to Zendik.

Details varied but not the bottom line, in ink still invisible to me: give it up or leave. "It" could be an inheritance, a car, a college fund. "It" could be good credit—on the Farm's behalf, some Zendiks accrued credit card debt that the Farm intended never to repay. Some gave it up with ease; some succumbed to pressure. A few—like the young woman who drove off in her milk-white four-door, rather than relinquish the title—resisted and left. I was unusual only in my quickness to anticipate the Farm's need.

My throat tightened, my heart pounded, as my balance shifted into Zendik's account. After Rayel clicked the receiver back into its cradle, a sagebrush waste opened in my gut and sent a scrubby, thorned grit-gust up through my ribs to my chest. Sure, I could still sleep at other communes—but only if I threw myself, penniless, on the mercy of the highway.

Early November, still. Late afternoon. I parked my wheelbarrow of split oak and pine by the Farmhouse porch, where Owen and I were stacking firewood between two posts. From the kitchen drifted the scent of cumin—dinner would be lentil patties with salad and yogurt sauce. From the Music Room rumbled the muffled thump of drums and bass, under Arol's improvised vocals, swinging from shrill to throaty to wistful. From the goat barn came the does' nasal whine-brays, raised against the affront of being locked in a stanchion. Red with the work of powering my load uphill from the woodpile, I set to piecing the fuel into a three-dimensional puzzle. Handing me the last chunk, Owen looked up from the barrow, as if a thought had just grabbed him by the blond curls dabbing his forehead. "Hey, Helen," he said, "did you know they have levels?"

"What are you *talking* about?"

I favored Owen over the rest of my roommates. If they were the trolls in my fairy tale, he was the elf. A psychedelics dealer from Charleston, South Carolina—a popular Zendik selling spot—he'd arrived in a Phish T-shirt printed with a ring of cotton candy–colored animals holding hands against a tie-dyed cumulous sky. He saw time as an ocean or a spiral; he reminded me that Y2K—just a couple months away—meant nothing according to the Mayan calendar, which revolved around the moon. Sometimes his eyes shone with the glow of waking trance. He said he'd had a revelation while speaking with Zendik sellers one night on Meeting Street: he was to break off his engagement and follow them home. That I believed. Revelations happened. But this business about levels? Nonsense. I'd been at the Farm at least a week longer than he had. How could he know something I didn't?

"You know those wristbands they all wear?"

I nodded. I *had* noticed the ragged strips of colored cloth circling the Zendiks' wrists—and dismissed them as adornment. I dropped the oak chunk into its rough nest.

"They show what level everybody's at."

I turned to look at him. He wasn't doing the waking-trance thing. His pupils were a normal size.

"That's ridiculous. Are you telling me this place has a *hierarchy?*"

He shrugged. "Hey, I'm just passing on what I heard." He glanced up the hill toward the barns. Toba was crunching down the gravel path. He tilted his head in her direction. "If you don't believe me, ask her."

He grabbed the barrow's handles and pushed off for the woodpile. I corralled Toba a few steps from the porch and spilled out his wristband story. "He's making that up, right?" I searched her eyes for a dismissive flicker. "I mean, it's not true—is it?"

She fingered a frayed end of the dusty-rose strip tied to her wrist. She nodded. "Yes, there are levels. Shown by the different colors."

The sagebrush waste in my gut sent up a fresh grit-gust. *Oh no.* Sure, I'd noticed that some Zendiks kept to the Mobile, even for meals; that I wasn't free to enter there without permission; that work assignments flowed downhill from the stubby house on stilts. Still, in the absence of clear tiering by grades or other measures, I'd assumed equality—something I thirsted for after years of being ranked.

"But why?" I asked Toba. "I thought the idea here was that we're all working together, that everyone cooperates to get things done. Now I feel like all of a sudden I'm at the bottom of some ladder I have to scramble to climb."

A tendon twitched in Toba's neck. She stilled it with a deep breath. Sandstone calm steadied her gaze. "Helen. There is no ladder. There is no hierarchy. It's not that some people are above others; it's just that some are more committed. They have more experience living the Zendik philosophy. That doesn't mean they get special privileges—it means they take more responsibility."

The grit-gust rose to my throat. "But . . . but . . . I *hate* that. I don't wanna live in a place with that kind of division."

"Listen," she said, "I know it's hard not to see Zendik through the lens of your competitive conditioning. I mean, you've been competing all your life. That's how you got through Harvard. That's what you *have* to do to survive in the Death-culture. Of course you're gonna make this another contest." She shrugged, as if to say *I'd* be the loser if I didn't believe her. "But it's not. We're coming from a totally different place."

A totally different place. A place whose story made sense to the rest of its inhabitants. For my story to match Zendik's, *mine* would have to change.

chapter 3

Dim Chambers

SHORTLY AFTER LEARNING WHAT the wristbands meant, I gained one of my own: green, for Zendik Apprentice, the bottom tier of the Zendik tower. Above me, in ascending order, were Kore Apprentices (brown), the Kore (royal blue), Family Apprentices (gray), and the Family (royal purple). Also above me, but shunted off to a scaffold hanging at no fixed height, were Family Warriors (dusty rose)—Zendiks who'd evolved to a certain level of consciousness, then stopped.

With my wristband I received a double-sided sheet, dense with single-spaced text, listing the criteria for reaching each level. This document, like most of the Zendik writing I'd read, lacked precision. It defined neither the mysterious process of "evolving" nor the elusive prize called "evolution." It did not explain how I could win a brown wristband, or a blue one; it did not light passages from one tier to the next. I assumed that the veteran Zendiks had developed the etheric equivalent of night vision, and that once I'd done the same, the hidden stairs and ladders would emerge from the shadows. In the meantime, I combined glances at Zendiks' wrists with what I knew of their histories to pick out patterns that seemed useful—if too superficial, I was sure, to reveal the *real* story.

Position in the hierarchy corresponded roughly to time spent at Zendik. A year or so earned you a brown wristband; two to four bumped you up to royal blue; five or six pushed you to gray; seven or more vaulted you to royal purple. But there were exceptions. The Farm's three children, all younger than seven, were in the Family. Prophet, the flint-chipped man I'd seen with Arol the day I'd met her, had been at the Farm only about a year; Lyrik, consort to Arol's daughter, Swan, had accrued about five years. Yet both wore royal purple. With no men matching Arol and Swan in status, I couldn't aspire to so swift an ascent. But I could find a lover a level or two above me to accelerate my climb. Estero's band of royal blue—hugging his oak-knot wristbones, kissing his olive skin—made him only more alluring.

By mid-November—despite my donation, my decision to stay, my acquisition of a wristband—I still hadn't earned a bunk in the Farmhouse. I hadn't even mounted the steps from the living room to the loft where the women slept. So I was torn—between fear and excitement—when Eile invited me, at lunch one day, into their sanctum. "The girls are all getting together for specs tonight. Do you wanna join us?"

I knew what "specs" were—Eile had already walked me through the Zendik protocol for birth control. I didn't know if I was ready to participate in, or witness, so intimate a ritual.

"Spec" was short for "speculum"—the tool Eile and her mentors, Shure and Loria, used to check Zendik females for signs of fertility before each date. If a woman's cervical fluid was clear and stretchy and her *os*, or cervical mouth, was open, then she couldn't "ball"—that is, have intercourse. As a backup,

Zendik women tracked their waking temperatures; a rise in temperature, sustained over a few days, indicated ovulation. At Eile's urging, I'd put a basal thermometer on the communal shopping list and begun recording my readings on a chart she'd given me. I wasn't aware that it was possible for women to check their own cervical fluid, and assess their own fertility, in private.

Nor was I aware—never having used a prophylactic other than abstinence—that some women might have preferred condoms to specs and thermometers. Zendiks didn't use condoms. Later, I would hear the cover story: condoms reduce pleasure and intimacy; pausing to apply one breaks lovemaking's flow. Later still, I would glimpse some of what this cover obscured: Wulf, who'd shunned condoms, had fucked most of the women on the Farm. Mandating fertility awareness helped prepare them to deliver the kind of sex he desired. (Five years after Wulf's death, Arol would finally approve limited condom use.) Further, specking reminded lovers that even in seclusion they were not alone: the tribe had penetrated the woman first; the tribe decided who had sex and who bred; the tribal eye saw all, even in the dark.

But it wasn't the tribal eye that prickled my spine with anxiety as I considered Eile's invite. It was my *own* eyes. Where would I rest them when the women dropped their pants to get specked? Would they all bare their crotches at once? Would they expect me to bare mine?

Sensing my apprehension, Eile flashed a reassuring smile. "You don't actually have to *get* specked if you don't want to. It's totally fine just to hang out, be social, watch how it works. You can try it yourself some other time."

I still didn't know where I'd rest my eyes. But it helped to hear I wouldn't need to drop my pants. And I wasn't about to pass on a chance to advance toward the Farm's heart. "Sure, I'll come," I said.

Climbing the stairs to the loft that night, warmed by the blaze in the woodstove, I took wistful note of all that was missing from my dorm in the barn: soft quilts and comforters draping the dozen or so beds; collages—of birds, jungles, sunsets, waterfalls—brightening the dark paneling; Oriental rugs cloaking the hardwood floor. In the corner farthest from the railing, lounging on a few beds in an oval of lamplight, were all the women on the Farm except Arol and Swan—about twenty in total.

Perched at the oval's edge, I watched as the others grabbed their speculums, each wrapped in a pretty scarf, from a green plastic basket stowed under Eile's bed. I watched as they took turns shedding jeans and underpants and stretching out on her quilted mattress, heads and shoulders propped by pillows, legs crooked and spread. Kneeling between their knees, she had them slide in the speculum and squeeze it open to afford her a flashlit glimpse of the *os*. Was it closed? Open? Slightly open? Next she used a Q-tip to retrieve a strand—or dab, or smudge—of cervical fluid. Was it clear and stretchy? White and sticky? White and creamy? Open and stretchy meant no balling. Closed and dry meant ball away. In-between states triggered questions—What day are you on? Has your temperature risen? How long's your average cycle?—and then a consultation with Shure, who'd been gauging fertility for about as long as Eile had been alive. Shure said yes or no when Eile couldn't decide.

As one woman after another received her verdict, those who'd finished or were waiting chatted about dates they'd had or were about to have, which positions brought the most pleasure, how to achieve the elusive Big O—orgasm from intercourse. I marveled at their ease: with words like "cock" and "box" and "fuck"; with their own and others' nudity; with sharing tips about sex. I still felt a jolt each time a woman dropped her pants—if she was going to bare one half of her body, shouldn't it be the top half?—but after the first few rounds I began to relax about where to rest my eyes. No one seemed to care.

When most of the women had taken their turns—and some, including Shure, had left the loft to go on dates or go to bed—Eile asked if I'd like to try. "No pressure," she said. "You totally don't have to if you don't feel comfortable. But it can be pretty wild to get a look at your *os* for the first time."

My bladder clenched, warning me I wasn't ready. I'd never even seen a gynecologist, never received this sort of exam before. In the next beat, I dismissed the warning as a drag on my ascent. "Why not?" I said, stepping toward the bed.

Eile fished a spare speculum out of the green basket. As I removed my pants and underpants and lay back on the bed, my bladder clenched again. But I couldn't pull out now, I told myself; I'd already chosen. I ignored the second warning.

I crooked my knees up and slid the clear plastic dolphin nose into my vagina. (At the time, I avoided naming this part of myself; soon I, too, would adopt the word "box.") Eile peered inside me, pointing her Mini Maglite down the tunnel opened by the dolphin nose. "You're not there," she said. "Aim up and to the left."

"There you are!" she said, after a few more stabs. "Do you wanna see yourself?"

"Okay."

She set a small mirror and the Maglite between my legs. I saw a glistening pink bump, pierced by a tiny slit. Not "wild," as Eile had promised—but new. A fresh item to add to my list of Things I Would Have Missed Had I Not Come to Zendik. A list that helped crowd out doubts—*I should have kept the money; I should have explored more before deciding to stay.*

Eile withdrew the light and mirror and inserted a Q-tip, which emerged with a touch of spongy mucus clinging to it. "Closed and slightly wet!" she said. A split verdict, in other words.

"Don't worry," she added. "Once you've charted a few cycles, we'll have more to go on." She smiled. "That's gonna matter a lot more once you start having dates."

Karma was lying on her stomach on the next bed over, head propped in her hands. She rolled onto her side and gave me a mischievous grin. "Speaking of dates!" she said. "Who are you attracted to?"

I ducked down to retrieve my clothing. A blush crept over my cheeks. My shoulder tingled with the imprint of Estero's awakening touch, my first morning at the Farm. His face—his mysterious smile, his serious gaze—shimmered in my mind's eye. I hesitated to say his name, for fear that Karma would scoff at me, confirm that he was out of my league.

I said it anyway: "Estero." Despite the strangeness of the scene, I felt warmth from Eile and Karma, their wish to see me blossom. "There are plenty of hot guys here, but he . . ." I paused, seeking a word or phrase to do his beauty justice. Finding none, I finished the sentence as best I could: "He is absolutely *gor*geous."

Karma laughed, her eyes alight with sly encouragement. "Go ahead and hit him up for a walk! All work and no play makes Helen a dull girl! Why not have a little fun, right? What have you got to lose?" Eile nodded. "Yeah, go for it."

"Maybe I will," I said. A seed of what might be settled within me.

I knew a few details of Estero's background from a letter published in the Zendik magazine before his 1997 move to the Farm. About quitting his $36,000-a-year job as an engineer for a multinational telecom giant, he'd written, "I didn't feel people needed more cellular phones, towers marking up the landscape, and more radio frequencies floating around. . . . I got sick of working, coming home to smoke pot and relax, going to sleep, and doing it all over again. It was going nowhere quick." At Zendik, he adopted the role of village electrician.

Now I recognize Estero's letter as the germ of his creation

myth. Every Zendik had one, running something like this: My world was brutish and dull. I had to numb myself to survive. At the Farm I found friendship and purpose. Finally I feel fully alive.

After less than a month's exposure to this story line, I was already drafting my own version: I graduated from Harvard with a grant to tour communal homesteads. For months I wandered, growing weary of groups that seemed bohemian but hadn't committed to cooperation and honesty. At Zendik I found a family, a tribe. Here I could develop not only skill and understanding but also an exceptional degree of intimacy, especially with men. (Surely all this was worth more than $13,000—right?)

Into my myth, I'd scripted a role for Estero: His kiss would transform me from shy, croaking frog to bold, lilting princess. He would rouse me to sensual pleasure, then guide me through sex. We'd cultivate a lasting love, rooted in our common devotion to Zendik.

But first I had to "hit him up." And even though Karma and Eile had been encouraging, I doubted he'd say yes.

Estero, I would learn, had been a child model. At twenty-five, he could have swung a Calvin Klein shoot—for a spread in *Mother Earth News*. He paired starved elegance and a soulful gaze with a homesteader's take on shabby chic: worn jeans, weathered cowboy boots, vintage olive drab vest screen-printed on the back with a faded logo for a faded Zendik project, the Ecolibrium Alliance. He was, simply, far hotter than I. The same was true of most every other woman within his mating circuit. I doubted my own voltage would be high enough to excite him.

But how could I know for sure, unless I took a chance? Telling myself I'd be foolish *not* to take advantage of access to go-betweens, I asked Loria, shortly after breakfast one day in late November, to hit up Estero for a walk on my behalf.

Then I waited. For the rest of the morning and the entire afternoon, I pulsed with a buzz both luscious and cruel—a cross between the caress of a vibrator and the zing of a weak electric fence. The day's work—shoveling horseshit, making salad, building a rock wall—morphed into a medium for the buzz, which dulled the pangs I sometimes felt for times in the past when I'd conducted my own orchestra, composed my own score. When I'd been free to read books, or sculpt with balloons, or walk twenty miles, or ride the F train in loops between Jamaica and Coney Island. Now, an unseen hand waved the baton. It could wave forever—I would follow—if I could sway in this buzz every once in a while.

I was at the kitchen counter, scooping rice into my dinner bowl, when Loria leaned in to ask if she might have a word with me in the freezer room. (Loria, an English heiress, could carry off phrases like "have a word with.") My heart gave a jolt. I stowed my bowl in a nook under a cupboard and followed her into the poorly lit alcove. Under a flickering bulb, her Marilyn Monroe lips stretched into a conspiratorial grin. "Estero is into it. You're to meet him at his shop around nine. Just knock on the door. He'll be there."

My heart gave another jolt. I grinned back at Loria. "Wow, that's so great! Thank you!"

She winked. "Of course. Enjoy yourself."

A few hours later, after showering and changing and reading a couple Wulf essays—to soothe myself, to purify my excitement over this walk into ardor for the bigger project of revolutionizing relationships—I stepped out of the Farmhouse living room and into the starry dark. As I climbed the hill toward the barns, a gentle breeze—infused with the sweet, grassy scents of cured alfalfa hay and fresh manure—skimmed the tips of my ears. Gravel crunched under my boots. Anticipation rinsed me in blissful dread, then thrust my heart into the rapid thump of its spin cycle.

Estero's shop—a long shed—was a few steps downhill from the goats' milking parlor. I cleared the rise and turned right. Beneath the door I was to knock on glowed a thin band of light. I stalled, seeking a cue in the string of thumps, taps, and clicks from within—until my fear of being caught wavering trumped my fear of stepping forth.

I knocked.

"Come in!"

Inside, Estero stood halfway down the shop's narrow aisle, probing the blade of an injured blender with a pair of pliers. I was glad the shop's lone bulb was trained on him; maybe he wouldn't notice my stiff stance, my deep flush. He grinned in welcome and told me to take a seat, he'd be finished in a minute. I sidled past him to perch on a bare patch of bench. I feigned interest in the set of socket wrenches hanging in ascending sizes from the pegboard across from me—while sneaking glances at that tangled ponytail, that elegant profile.

He gave the blade a final twist and set down the pliers. "Shall we go?" he asked.

"Sure," I croaked.

We strolled down the hill, past the sloping goat barn, through the salvage yard, past the largest and most prolific wild persimmon tree on the property. By now, most of the fruit, tinged purple, had dropped to the grass and split open, oozing cinnamon, caramel, citrus, winter. We followed a faint trail into a meadow where the does sometimes browsed, then picked a path through the hummocky waste where we'd one day dig a pond. Beyond us loomed Wildcat Spur—our mountain bulwark, home to the highest point in Polk County.

As we walked, I asked Estero for his past, holding back what I already knew from the letter I'd read. I gleaned a couple more details: he'd grown up in rural Illinois and attended technical college in Indianapolis before securing the job he'd quit to come to Zendik. I asked for his future: Did he see the Farm as his permanent home? He nodded, casting his eyes, ridge to ridge, across the sky. "I can't imagine being anywhere else."

He took my hand. He was *holding my hand*. Palm to palm, callus to callus, his knuckles a miracle under my fingertips.

I couldn't imagine being anywhere else either.

I reciprocated with my own myth, shaping our walk into its latest chapter. In a Wulf essay I'd read and reread, "Friendship unto Love," he'd laid out the four stages of romantic partnership: Work, Respect, Friendship, Love. If a union was to last, he said, it had to begin in the Work of building the Zendik movement. Through Working together, the lovers developed Respect for each other. Respect made way for Friendship— full knowledge and acceptance of the other—which in turn made way for Love. A special, ineffable Zendik kind of love. Unavailable elsewhere. Before Zendik, I told Estero, I'd flailed at mating: shy of approaching guys I liked, I'd taken touch where I could get it. This walk, right now, was my first intimate encounter with a man I respected and hoped to know forever.

How could I have made such a declaration without sounding ridiculously earnest? Maybe that's how I *did* sound. Maybe Estero was chuckling into his vest collar as I spoke. Maybe the grunts of the bucks, in their pen across the creek, drowned his chuckle out.

By this time, we'd traced most of a lasso-shaped loop through the hintermeadows and the lower field. We were back in the salvage yard—known as the "wood yard" for the towering iron racks of neatly sorted boards that dwarfed the heaps of sinks and pipes, the stacks of bricks and cinder blocks. Estero led me halfway up the slope, then shrugged his vest off and spread it on the ground to shield my back from the bumpy damp. He reclined beside me. We stared up at the stars. There, again, was the belt of Orion. He slid his arm around my shoulders. I wanted it there. Yet I flinched. He turned to me and smiled. "You're a virgin, right?"

"How'd you know?"

"Loria told me." He squeezed my shoulder. "It's okay, I know you wanna take it slow. You can relax with me. I promise."

I believed him. Yet I couldn't relax. I shook with tension and cold.

Estero helped me to my feet, donned his vest, and led me up the slope to a level spot above the burn pile. He pulled me close—chest to chest, hip to hip, thigh to thigh. The shaking stopped, as I sucked in all the warmth I wanted. Then he leaned in to kiss me—and set off the electric rush.

It flashed loose through my body. Jolts of hot joy coursed through my throat, chest, crotch, toes. I felt as if I'd descended to the subway tracks where male meets female and stumbled on the third rail.

Maybe the electric rush erupted from a difference in charge. Maybe it fed on my nervous excitement, my weeks of daydreaming, my hunger, after years of near chastity, for physical love. Maybe I'd just gotten lucky.

But these were not the stories I told myself as I stood, tingling, in Estero's embrace.

In "Friendship unto Love," Wulf had said, "Until you have loved and made love with another who shares precisely your Cosmic Responsibility, you have only loved with the eyes and the body, never the mind, never the intelligence, never the total organism, the total Self." This, I thought, was the first time I'd kissed a man with my "total Self." *That* was the source of my pleasure. That, and the fact that Estero and I—as my myth had predicted—were *meant for each other.*

I gazed up at him and grinned, belly and hips pressed against his, chest swelling with another earnest declaration. "I can't believe how good this feels," I said.

He blinked, and smiled back, but not as widely as I had. A soft breeze dusted us with the burn pile's ashy musk.

Too soon, Estero pulled free. "It's getting late," he said. I nodded, though "late" meant nothing to me. Had it been an hour—two hours? more?—since I'd knocked on his door? Time had turned into a thing that stretched and shimmered, like the cloud of possibility hovering around us. I would have pulsed in his orbit till dawn, had he allowed it.

Instead I spun fantasies of what might happen when I saw him in the morning. I'd seen other pairs of lovers eat their breakfast hip to hip, nuzzle on the couch, share a lingering embrace before heading off to separate work crews. Yes, big chunks of intimate time had to be scheduled—but couples who dug each other enough found ways to intertwine in the interstices.

I was baffled when Estero dispatched me with a brisk hug and quick kiss in the living room before dashing off to install outlets in the Bathhouse. Couldn't he tell that something wondrous had begun? Or had the electric rush been running a closed circuit within my insulating skin?

That evening, after spilling my confusion to Luya—the only other female Zendik Apprentice—I knocked on Estero's door again. I said what she'd suggested: that I'd really liked our walk and wanted to "make contact." He set his pliers down, strode to the doorway, and ringed me in his arms. We kissed; the electric rush surged through me, stronger than before. Then he sent me off, saying he had to get back to work. I knew, deep down, that love makes time elastic. That if he'd shared my feelings *he* would have sought *me* out. For the time being, though, I'd leave those thoughts in shadow. I'd keep that trap door closed.

The first week of December, I got what I'd wanted since my first night at the Farm: a bunk with the other women, in their dorm above the living room. But it came with complications.

A few weeks earlier, I'd escaped the plywood box full of new guys—but not by much. Luya had invited me to take the bunk above hers, in the main part of the barn loft. We were the only two women in a dorm full of men. Luya had joined the Zendiks at their Texas location a few years earlier, staying long enough to prove her value as a "power seller"—someone who consistently raked in big bucks on selling trips. But her departure had dropped her to the bottom tier of the tower. She'd had to prove herself all over again after returning to the Farm in North Carolina.

The original invitation to ascend to the Farmhouse had been issued exclusively to Luya. But she'd demurred, insisting to the other women that they'd lose me if they didn't bring me in from the barn. Though it's hard to imagine a Zendik Apprentice exerting pressure on Kore Apprentices and Kore members, she did win me a space in the Farmhouse by refusing to move without me.

By this time, the upstairs room was no longer a loft; a wall had replaced the railing. Still, there was no room for an extra bedstead. So I was given a plywood platform, maybe eight by eight feet, under the ceiling—a tiny, nosebleed A-frame, installed just for me. For some reason, I called it my bat cave. To reach my cave, I climbed a ladder that one of the carpenters had fashioned from two-by-fours. To conserve floor space, he'd made it strictly vertical. I had to watch my step to avoid falling off.

At its peak, my bat cave gave me only about four feet of headroom. I didn't want to shrink this with a mattress. And I didn't mind lying on hard surfaces. So I rolled my sleeping bag out on the plywood. My new roommates made good-natured fun of my ascetic bent: "She sleeps on a *board*," they said.

When I lay on my back and looked up, I saw a swarm of ladybugs. Hundreds of them. They'd made a home in the seam at the peak of the ceiling. They smelled like steam-heated iron filings. I watched with a mix of fascination and revulsion the scurry and pulse of their communal life. Sometimes they lost their grip; I never got used to the tiny plunk of a bug on my face as I waited for sleep. But I did make peace with their presence. I did come to appreciate their fecundity, their vigor, their industry.

When I sat up on my board and looked out, I saw Jayd. Her bat cave, at the far end of the room, was the mirror image of mine. There couldn't have been less than ten feet between our two ladders, yet, in my memory, she's so close I can see the sparkles in her lavender nail polish. Through no fault of her own, her nearness oppressed me.

Jayd, seventeen, had been at the Farm about a year, to my month and a half. She wore the brown wristband of the Kore Apprentice and regularly went selling. She *was* unusually young for a Zendik, but she wasn't the only one who'd exchanged a chaotic life on the street, or a struggle with drugs, or an abusive family, for the relative calm and security of the Farm. Zar, a Family member who'd fathered Arol and Wulf's first grandchild, had left his LA street gang for Zendik at sixteen. Zar's current girlfriend, Donna, had been the same age when she'd hitched a ride back to the Farm with a selling crew she'd met at a Phish show.

Jayd may have mentioned the skirmish with despair and suicide that had driven her to Zendik. If she had, it hadn't roused my empathy. Privately, spitefully, I condemned her languor on work crews, her dyed-black hair (wasn't hair dye of the Deathculture?), her adenoidal intonation—when really what bugged me was her closeness to Estero.

If I knew of their interest in each other before hitting on him, I dismissed it. The Zendik dating game *encouraged* players to switch partners, with its one-night limit. It was only after our walk that I sat up and took notice. How could I maintain my fantasy that he was as smitten with me as I was with him, when he kept hitting on Jayd?

In some other milieu, I might not have persisted (I might not have pursued Estero in the first place). But Zendik had twisted my mating story into a psychedelic swirl. In an essay called "Couples in Ecolibrium," Wulf advised against depending on any one person to meet every emotional need. While he admitted that a member of a Zendik couple might "[w]ant to sleep with that person, nobody else, want to have sex with that person, nobody else, want to have children with that person, nobody else," he warned that "then they might want to be totally intimate with that person, nobody else. That'll never work. They must commit to being totally intimate with the group, be total Zendiks in Ecolibrium." Elsewhere he said, "Love is interest, Love is attention, Love is fascination—fascination with the Love object—such fascination that there can be no place for the competitive attitudes and actions of rivalry, envy, jealousy." So dyads threatened the tribe, and what I felt for Estero must not be Love with a capital "L," since I was finding plenty of room for envy. How was I to coax a plot from this pulsing spiral of doctrine and desire?

One evening a week or so after that first walk, my frustration burst into words. Loria had just told me that Estero had refused my second hit-up, as he was already set to get together with Jayd. Blood rushed to my cheeks, crushing my guard. "I don't know what to do," I said. "I get so jealous whenever I see him with her or hear they're having a date. My instant reaction is, 'I hate her.'"

In the bathroom, the shower hissed on. Loria pursed her Marilyn Monroe lips and tucked a blond curl behind her ear. "You have to develop a revolutionary attitude toward relationships," she said. "Jealousy is just a conditioned reflex. It's how people react in a competitive culture. Here, you can relax." She paused. I nodded. "Ideally your interest in Estero would bring you and Jayd together. It's something you have in common. Why not use it as a starting point for friendship?" She smiled, flashing her broad band of perfect teeth. "Why not talk to *her* about it?"

Because I would feel horribly embarrassed. Because she *might not want to talk to* me.

A savvy girlfriend in the outside world might have advised me to forget Estero and find a guy who *liked* me. But Loria—a

Family member who'd spent more than a decade at the Farm, and years as Wulf's lover—had grown used to the contortions born of conforming your longings to another's ideal. The ideal *we* were thrashing toward had been conceived by Arol and Wulf and encoded in Zendik's own creation myth.

Carol Merson met Wulf Zendik (formerly Lawrence Wulfing) in Los Angeles in 1962, when she was twenty-three and he was forty-two. She'd just landed a part in a new TV series; he was writing fiction and poetry and dreaming of a lifelong partnership based on complete honesty. "In a square, old Society relationship," he wrote, "you can't even get to know each other because the other person is so valuable as a possession, as a shield against the madness and the insanity of the Deathculture. Everything is a defense against a hateful society . . . that is out to do you in." Enthralled by his vision and brilliance, and the promise of a life immersed in Love and Art, she ditched the acting job to be with him. She dropped the "C" from her first name and took the last name Wulf.

The two began playing music at clubs and cafes in LA. (Wulf, a seasoned performer, taught Arol to play along.) But the gigs didn't pay much. So Arol took up exotic dancing to cover food and rent—even though the late nights left her with little time or verve for art. Seeing that plenty of other artists were also struggling to get by, they imagined convening a tribe to share the burden of survival—a supportive social matrix in which people could do work they cared about, own and meet their true needs, and join Wulf and Arol in their quest to be honest. By this time, they'd realized that they could achieve complete honesty as a couple only within a community that shared their ideal.

Wulf's parents offered him and Arol the use of a ranch they owned in the high desert east of Los Angeles. They could do as they pleased with the place, as long as they maintained it and kept the taxes paid. In 1969, the pair relocated to the ranch and began to attract would-be communards from far and wide. They started growing their own food and formed a band that toured nearby colleges. Zendik Farm was born.

Coming together as a tribe meant confronting the lust to possess others, especially as lovers. "Possessive attitudes about sex," Wulf wrote, "lead to jealousy, hostility, hate, violence, murder." And such attitudes were vestigial if, as Wulf and Arol did, you defined love as interest, which didn't have built-in limits—just as you could be interested in multiple ideas or art forms, you could be interested in multiple people.

In 2006, Swan, nearing thirty, would offer this description of her parents' arrangement to a reporter from the *Washington Post*: "I grew up very strangely. . . . Mom and Dad, their relationship was sexually open from the beginning. They always had other lovers. I never remember them sleeping in the same bed. I grew up with Mom and Dad as Mom and Dad, and they were never together." That is, they were bound by a tie more advanced than monogamy: devotion to each other's evolution. The dauntless pursuit of Truth. Determination to create a cooperative, honest culture for Swan that would one day embrace all children. Their union—which lasted till Wulf's death in June 1999—was the nucleus of a relationship revolution that would heal humanity and the planet. It was the only example we had— the first instance in history—of Friendship unto Love.

If we followed it, we could help end the war between the sexes, wars among nations, the war on our precious web of life. We could hope to know enduring love. And we could expect to struggle long and hard: Wulf and Arol had fought their Death-culture conditioning for decades.

Of course I would balk at the thought of talking to Jayd about Estero. I'd been absorbing "possessive attitudes" for nearly twenty-three years.

The morning after I vented to Loria, I caught Jayd in her bat cave, applying makeup (wasn't makeup, like hair dye, the stain of the Deathculture?). Hunched at the lip of my bunk, I spilled out my envy: how rough it was to watch Estero climb her ladder for a kiss, how agonizing to fall asleep knowing they were naked nearby. Engulfed by my need to *tell*, I cast aside consideration of what she might want to *hear*. "Do *you* ever feel like that?" I asked. "Do you know what I mean?"

She lifted the hand mirror resting in her lap and resumed squinting into it. "Not really," she said, rimming her eyes with black liner.

I withdrew to the rear of my cave and gazed up at the ladybugs. *They* didn't doubt their desires or hang back in sacrifice. They crawled over and around each other if they had to. Plan B hatched as I watched them.

A couple nights later, I was back on Eile's bed, peeling a once-black tube sock off my speculum. (Finding no pretty scarves in the laundry-room giveaway bin, I'd settled for the faded, mateless sock.) Earlier that day, Estero had said yes to my request for a date. A real date. Complete with nakedness. Not a walk.

Eile drew a Q-tip out of my box and switched off her flashlight. "Open and stretchy! No fucking for you tonight." She sat down on the bed. "But you wouldn't be ready to ball yet anyway, right? It's gonna take a couple months for us to get to know your cycle."

"Right," I said. "I was figuring we'd just make out and get naked and stuff."

Eile grinned. "This is your first date, right? Are you nervous? Excited?"

I nodded and grinned back at her. But "nervous" and "excited" didn't begin to describe how I felt. More like in every cell electrified, tingling with desire to touch and be touched, gobsmacked by my glorious good luck.

On one score, though, I was *not* feeling lucky. I'd hoped to get together with Estero in one of the three tiny cabins—"date spaces"—the Zendiks had built especially for dates. Each cabin—just big enough for a double bed and a nightstand—was sided with mill ends and tucked among trees. I'd helped clean two of the three—the one by the Music Room and the one behind the horse barn (the one behind the Addition, I sensed, was off-limits). I loved the tie-dyed cotton curtains, the curlicued iron candleholders, the lengths of sateen and velveteen draping the walls and ceilings. I could imagine Sleeping Beauty waking in one of them, to the kiss of her prince.

Alas, that night in early December, all the cabins had gone to couples whose combined seniority trumped Estero's and mine. We'd been assigned to the trailer, a ratty clash of white metal parked a few paces from the woods, downslope from the Farmhouse. The interior pulsed with shades of red: maroon walls, crimson carpet, burgundy curtains. An overhead bulb shone through a lens littered with dead insects. Estero switched on the heater, lit candles, and darkened the bulb while I shrouded the stained gray mattress—resting on the floor—with my flower-print, queen-size "date sheet." (Each Zendik woman kept one of these and made sure it got washed between dates.) The reds receded into shadow. We removed our socks and shoes and dropped to the bed, where we sat—cross-legged, awkward—facing each other.

I was expecting Estero—Kore Zendik, fairy-tale prince, seasoned lover—to slowly, sensually undress me, kissing and caressing each newly revealed curve and crevice of my body. Instead, after fifteen minutes or so of kissing and groping, he asked, flat out, "Do you wanna take our clothes off?"

This was not the best use of open and honest communication, in my opinion, but I agreed anyway. We each disrobed separately.

It was a relief to be naked, to press the length of my limbs against the length of his. Twined together in bed, we traded sexual secrets, dissolving their shame in laughter. He confessed to fucking sheep in the fields of the farm where he'd grown up, and I recounted how I'd achieved my best solo orgasm ever: by blowing up one of those sausage-link balloon-animal balloons (using a special handheld pump) while it was inside me. (As a sculpture student working in the medium of inflatable latex, I'd taken inspiration from the art materials cluttering my dorm room.) I'd never told this story before, yet I didn't mind telling him. He had perversions of his own, and no clothes on, and we, like Arol and Wulf, were pushing each other to become more honest.

After a while we fell silent, and Estero slid down to my crotch to give me head. Again, I was expecting to be transported by his sensual powers. Maybe, despite the release of sharing secrets, I was too tense for pleasure; my orgasm that night was a blip, compared with the one I'd summoned via balloon and hand pump. Still, I was thrilled just to laze in Estero's embrace, to smooth the fine tangle of his hair—unbound, for once—and trace his elbows with my thumbs. I could not imagine ever growing tired of lying with him.

Again, he was the one to end it. Around midnight, after drifting off for a moment, he yawned, stretched, sat up. "I think it's time to turn in," he said.

As I dressed, I stiffened. By the time my shoes were tied, I'd lost the grace of feeling wanted. I hadn't prepared myself for this moment. Maybe deep down I'd been hoping that baring ourselves to each other would show Estero he was meant for me and wean him off polyamory. Even as I aspired to the ideal of a soul union transcending possession, I craved a love that wove through every day. A bond not snipped at the end of each date. I sensed that shared regard—despite the supposed supremacy of honesty—took the same forms here as it did in the "square" world: sitting close at meals; finding ways to work and play together; persevering even if the group disapproved; pausing to hug, kiss, talk.

Walking back to the Farmhouse, we stopped at the unfinished Bathhouse so Estero could test some wiring he'd installed earlier that day. I didn't care about the wiring; I did want to prolong our last moments alone. So I followed him up the makeshift cinder-block steps into the dark building, minding the wide gap between the threshold and the top block.

On my way out, I forgot the gap and tumbled out of the building onto the grass. Estero pulled me up and asked if I was okay, and of course I said yes, I was fine, no scrapes or breaks—maybe a bruise or two from bumping the blocks—but really I was grieving the ease I'd felt in the date space, cursing the rift already yawning between us, even as I savored what the fall had won me: one last touch.

The blessing, for an obsessed person, of living communally: you never know when you might run into your crush. The curse, for an obsessed person, of living communally: you never know when you might run into your crush.

After my date with Estero, I tried to revert to my pre-Zendik story of how to act in the presence of attractive men: Avoid eye contact. Sheen yourself in silence. Attend to something else.

My body refused to obey.

Grating carrots for salad one morning, I caught a swing of the screen door and a flash of olive drab out the corner of my eye. I stared into the salad bowl, intent on the pointed orange matchsticks tumbling from the teeth of the mandoline (which other Zendiks had nicknamed the finger-fucker). Then: the tap of boot heels on the hardwood floor behind me. And a bright red smear on the mint-green instrument, from a nick to my thumb.

Making a sign in the living room one evening, a box of markers at my hip and a pad of paper on my lap, I caught a flash of denim-clad knees, then the click of the side door. The pad lurched off my lap; the markers rolled everywhere. Crawling under the desk to retrieve some of them, I yanked the phone cord. The phone clattered to the floor.

Another morning, a week or so after the date, I was preparing to climb down from my bat cave when Loria rushed in to relay a hit-up from Estero—for Jayd. I missed the ladder and dropped straight down, knocking skull against hardwood. I sat up and clutched the hurt part. *I have to do something*, I thought, *or it's only gonna get worse.*

A couple days later, at lunchtime, I spotted Estero in the laundry room, head bent toward the drum of a bum washing machine. The laundry room was small, with lots of windows but only one door. I could see he was alone. I slipped in beside him. He couldn't slip out.

"Estero," I said, "can I ask you something?"

He straightened, startled, then turned to me and smiled. "Sure."

"How's it possible that you can like Jayd and me at the same time?"

He leaned against the shelves—of sheets, candles, lightbulbs, matches—that lined the shed's back wall. He slid his hands into his front pockets and met my gaze. "I get different things from each of you. You're totally different people."

"Yeah? Like what? What do you like about me?" I was hoping for a comment on how *he* felt when our limbs intertwined—for a hint, however faint, that his cells had picked up on the current that ran through mine.

"You're really smart," he said. "And you have beautiful eyes."

I nodded, even as I grew more bewildered. What did eyes and smarts have to do with touch and lust and sex? If that was how he really felt, *why had he said yes?*

Maybe he craved sexual variety. Maybe I was unwittingly helping him and Jayd stave off the quiz of death I would eventually hear Arol administer to couples who'd grown too close for her comfort: "If all you two care about is fucking each other, what are you doing here? Why don't you get the hell out and *get an apartment?*" But I was looking for a more esoteric explanation. Surely Estero must be acting on special knowledge accrued in his two years at Zendik. Maybe he'd taken the concept of love as interest—which I accepted only intellectually—and worked it into his body.

I wondered if I, too, could sustain multiple attractions, get different things from different lovers.

The next weekend, while Estero was selling in Florida, I arranged to go on a walk with Taridon, another Kore member. Well over six feet tall, with a straight blond mane that fell to his waist, he was a powerhouse among "power sellers," happiest when hoisting a standard and setting off on crusade. He didn't enrapture me, as Estero did. But I admired his status, his stature, his selling prowess. And he was handsome enough.

With Taridon, I once again traced a lasso-shaped loop through the wood yard and fields and back to the wood yard, where we stopped in the lee of the towering racks to kiss by starlight. There was warmth between us, but no electric rush. I concluded that, yes, I could enjoy the touch of a second choice—but not without aching for the one who came first.

chapter 4

The Lure of the Ring

I STOOD AT THE CENTER OF the dance room, ringed by sixty other Zendiks, about to take my vow. Earlier that night, all of us had showered and exchanged work clothes for our version of finery: slacks, button-down shirts, skirts and dresses, tunics and blouses. Silk and twill, velvet and satin. We'd been told to dress up in dark colors for our consecration as warriors. Our racing pulse repelled the winter chill.

It was December 31, 1999. A few minutes to midnight. Most had already spoken; we would finish our ritual before the millennium turned. And then? *Let* Y2Chaos storm the Death-culture. We told our own stories; we kept our own time.

Arol, up in the Addition, watching the Farm's three children, was the one adult who would not stand where I stood.

I'd practiced the vow dozens of times aloud, and countless times in silence, to make sure I'd perform it perfectly, despite my nerves. I took a breath and spoke the first of three parts: "As a Zendik Warrior, I place mySelf on the Truthway and vow my Life and loyalty to this revolution of conscience and consciousness."

To my right was a small table laden with necklaces. Behind it stood Swan—mistress of ceremonies and, to me, Cinderella perpetually at the ball. The dance room had been built for her; here she practiced and sometimes led classes. Immaculately groomed and beautifully garbed, she seemed to travel in her own galaxy of rose scent and smooth sparkle. She had blue eyes, and blond curls kinked like coral. Though dark roots peeked out even then, it would take me years to realize that her hair, beneath its gold veneer, was brown like mine.

Though just six months my senior and also a fire dragon by the Chinese calendar, Swan ranged ages ahead of me on the Zendik evolutionary scale. If she was a mammal, endowed with higher-order thinking skills and milk for her young, then I was a protozoan, just growing used to my nucleus. Born to Arol and Wulf in June 1976—seven years after they'd started the Farm—she was the first child to know only cooperation and honesty. The first dancer—the first artist—to develop her genius unfettered. She had never, her creation myth held, suffered corruption by the Deathculture. No wonder I wished I could turn back the clock and sneak into Arol's womb next to her.

That night, thanks to my roommates, I reflected a glint of Swan's sparkle. Eile had lent me a pair of silver hoops set with violet rhinestones—the first earrings I'd worn in years—to complement the navy blouse and slim-fitting velvet jacket that Riven, a Kore Apprentice, had pulled from her shelves.

I clasped my hands behind my back, then dropped them to my sides. Staring straight ahead, I channeled the current of excitement in the room without meeting any one gaze. The ring of Zendiks faded into a pulsing haze. Two months earlier, I would have dismissed the vow as so much mumbo-jumbo; by now I was practiced at casting vagueness as portent and bringing my own meaning. I saw myself stepping through a fiery eye into a sphere of pure surrender as I spoke the second part:

"I vow to become Affirmative in all I find true about mySelf, my world, and the Universe itSelf."

Most Zendiks, including me, had a copy of "The Affirmative Life," a paperback booklet of Wulf quotes small enough to slip in a back pocket. Each page offered either a reminder of cosmic connection ("I am the Mortal Manifestation of Infinite Mind and I carry the Great Spirit within me . . .") or a whippet of metaphysical life coaching ("Dare to demand the Impossible and it becomes Possible," "Feel the Glory of Simply Being Alive"). We treated it like an oracle, choosing a random page and trusting it to yield just the right insight.

The source material for "The Affirmative Life"—Wulf's raps (talks) and writings on the subject—took a harsher tone than the sayings in the booklet. In a piece titled "Affirmative Living," Wulf said, "When and if you should catch yourSelf in negative moods of any form, cease it instantly, for it is a virulent toxin and will surely sicken and kill you. . . . No one gets away with anything in this Life. No act of criminal negativity will go unpunished." But I still imagined that affirmative living would lead me toward ever greater well-being and understanding. I'd yet to be charged with "criminal negativity," shocked by Zendik's emotional electric fence.

"To all Zendik Warriors, I place mySelf by your side as a weapon in our righteous fight to victory."

That was it. I'd recited each word just right. The haze resolved once again into a ring of Zendiks. How thrilled I was to join my fate with theirs.

I turned to face Swan. From the heap, she plucked a necklace: an amulet strung on a slender rope of twined floss. Each amulet, hammered and soldered by two of the Zendik men, was identical: a copper Z in a brass circle. The circle-Zs, unlike the wristbands, would mark us to outsiders—set us apart in our war for a beautiful world.

Flushed with the heat of sixty beating hearts, I bent my head and stretched it forward. She looped the rope around my neck.

Kro lay on his side, head propped in his hand. I sat cross-legged, facing him, my date sheet swaddling the thin mattress he'd dragged down from the barn loft to the parking lot and installed in the back of the green van—on a busy night in mid-January, our best bet for a date space.

We'd been hanging out—in roughly these positions—for more than an hour, warmed by a heater plugged into the van's cigarette lighter. Candlelight glinted off Kro's circle-Z pendant and mine, reminding us that our date served a purpose higher than our own pleasure: We were Zendik Warriors. Our relationships were battlefields in the fight between Truth and Lie. Every move we made either slowed or sped humanity's march toward ecocide.

So I was jarred, but not surprised, when Kro delivered a variation on the first lines of one of my favorite songs, the Meat Loaf ballad "Two Out of Three Ain't Bad." Lifting his head from his hand, he said, "Look, we could talk all night. But that's not what we're here for. How about we get on with it?"

I nodded. I uncrossed my legs, breaking the membrane of my comfort zone.

I liked Kro and respected his intellect. He was better read, and a better writer, than most of the Zendiks. With them, I simplified my diction to fend off taunts about "big words" and "Harvard"; with him, I didn't have to. And I appreciated the work he'd done, in the handful of Zendik philosophy classes he'd led for me and the new guys, to clarify Wulf's murky prose.

Kro's rapport with Wulf, as a thinker, anchored his Zendik creation myth: A decade earlier, at a taping of Wulf's public-access TV show in Austin, Wulf had called Kro onstage and talked with him the entire half hour. That meeting had inspired Kro to quit his job as an aide at the Texas School for the Deaf and move to the Farm. He would eventually win a commission from Arol to write essays for the website on Wulf's life and historical context—to render his legend for the layman.

Later, I would learn that Zylem, the veteran Zendik who'd taken my phone call about visiting, had woven Kro into *my* creation myth. I'd arrived at the Farm just three days after Kro's thirty-fourth birthday. This synchronicity, plus our intellectual affinity, had led Zylem to suggest to Kro that he'd psychically summoned me. That he and I were meant to be.

Yet I didn't find Kro attractive. He hunched when he walked, as if to make himself smaller; he seemed to shrink inside his tall, broad, potentially powerful body, like a shut-in confined to a few rooms of his home. His hairline, too, was receding, enlarging his already high forehead. Unlike Estero— whom I'd yet to give up on—Kro had not modeled as a child. And he was eleven years older than I was.

So why did I go on a date with him? Because he asked— he was the first Zendik to hit *me* up. Because he wore the royal blue wristband of the Kore and I, still with green around my wrist, was flattered by his interest. (Since his initial arrival in 1990, Kro had left the Farm twice, and twice returned; his current stint was in its third year.) Because Estero's indifference was leaving me hungry and I was eager to try the varieties of sexual experience. Because Wulf had said, in "The Affirmative Life," "All Power awaits your Yes."

Wulf had also said that sex was vital to evolutionary ascent: "We fuck our way to Paradise or there is no Paradise. No one ascends to that Divine plane of Enlightenment who remains sensually censored." Uncrossing my legs in the green van, I chose to interpret the lurch in my gut as sensual censorship and override it. I straightened my knees and stretched out beside Kro. I liked how his heft made me feel delicate.

His lips on mine tasted like a creosote bush smells—a blend of beans and incense. If Estero's touch sizzled with electricity, Kro's gave off the steady warmth of a woodstove. Maybe that was why I didn't tense when he slipped my pants off and went to give me head. Ease bred pleasure. I twisted my hips in rhythm with his tongue, as it lolled and rolled and licked and tumbled. (I'd understand later, with greater experience, that Kro was that rare jewel among men: one who delighted in giving head and was exceptionally good at it.) I broke the silence I'd learned as a college student masturbating behind thin dorm walls to emit the occasional moan. And when I reached orgasm—the first good one I hadn't given myself—I saw clouds parting in a pale sky. I'd never felt so clear, so bodily appreciated, with a man before.

In the wake of my date with Kro, I hoped the clarity I'd found with him would carry over to dates with Estero. It didn't. I concluded I would feel it only when a man gave me his full attention—when his gaze and touch told me I was the one he desired most. Each time I saw clouds part with Kro, a fresh rain doused the torch I bore for Estero.

By late February, I'd charted enough cycles to know I couldn't get pregnant in the first few days after my period. I'd also absorbed the Zendik imperative to "communicate"— *not* seeking advance feedback on your plans meant you were a "loner," locked in the Deathculture pattern of "running your own show." Surely, having sex for the first time was too big a leap to take on my own.

I'd need permission. Which was what I was seeking when I squeezed onto the last spot of bare floor near the front and center of the quickly filling living room, one night when I knew I wasn't fertile and was set to get together with Kro. Just a few yards away, claiming an entire couch, sat Zar, the Family member with the power to say yes or no.

I'd tried to get cleared for sex by a woman, in a more private setting. But when I'd put my request to Rayel, in the kitchen before dinner, she'd advised me to ask Zar at the sex meeting instead. I didn't see why she'd defer to him—she, too, wore a purple wristband—but I wasn't about to challenge her judgment. So I recast my nerve-racking task as a chance to enact the promise of Karma's Woodstock story: that here I could pursue sex openly, with the blessing of my community.

I knew how sex meetings worked, since I'd been to a couple already in my four months at the Farm: With Zar presiding, lower-level Zendiks took turns spilling their sexual struggles. He might give feedback of his own; he might solicit it from others in the Family or from the group as a whole. Sometimes the subject's face lit up as she listened. More often it burned with embarrassment or crumpled like paper held to flame. Though Arol sometimes mentioned issues raised at these meetings, she did not attend.

Zar sat with knees apart and brawny, tattooed arms crossed over his broad chest. Chin raised in challenge, he scanned the crowd, quick with apprehensive chatter.

Zar, now pushing thirty, had moved to the Farm from Los Angeles at sixteen. In a magazine piece titled "Zar's Story," he'd laid out the Deathculture tribulations that had readied him for the redemption pledged by Zendik: His parents divorced when he was two. His dad died of cancer when he was six. His grandfather molested him when he was little, then hanged himself when Zar was twelve. To vent his latent rage at life, Zar clogged the toilets in his school's bathroom, causing a flood, and "beat the shit out of" a kid who'd insulted his grandfather. He flipped through his first porn mag at twelve and ran away to Hollywood at thirteen. There he joined a gang, shot speed, and got used to violence: he "was beaten up and did a lot of beating, too." A drug arrest at fourteen landed him in detention, then a rehab program that treated him with heavy sedation. At that point, he said, "I didn't give a fuck about anything. I had no hopes, no goals. . . . I knew it was all a lie, their whole stupid world. I couldn't join that. I bailed, came to the Farm."

At Zendik—then located in Boulevard, near San Diego—Zar found hip, hard-line surrogate parents in Arol and Wulf. He took up music, sculpting, and drawing while learning welding, knife making, and mechanics. He spent a few years in a relationship with Swan, who gave birth to their son when he was twenty-three and she was seventeen. His myth cast him as a diamond in the rough—a troubled kid whose move to Zendik had revealed him as a fine young man.

Zar never said what qualified him to lead a sex meeting. I assumed his authority flowed from his time with Swan—the one adult Zendik whose sexuality had not suffered corruption by the Deathculture—and his reputation as a virtuoso lover who'd try anything to pleasure a partner. Now I see his credentials more clearly. His air of menace. His bond with Arol. She could trust him to snuff errant sparks, then lead her to the tinder.

Zar cleared his throat and surveyed the thicket of faces tilted up at him. The talk stopped. The room stilled. A sardonic half grin deepened the knife scar on his right cheek. "So. Does anybody have any questions?"

A dozen hands shot up. Zar pointed to Blayz, a Kore Apprentice. Six five and ripped, Blayz stood a good foot taller than Zar—but not when he was cross-legged on the floor, a few steps from Zar's feet.

"I haven't had sex in eight months," said Blayz, "and I'm just so fucking frustrated." He scowled. "I keep trying, but all the girls say no when I hit them up. I don't know what to do. I just wanna have sex. With *some*body."

Eight months earlier—before my arrival—Blayz and Teal had broken up, under pressure. Most likely they'd been found guilty of the usual charges: You're in a bubble. You're fucking with our survival. If you can't commit—*first*—to the revolution, you don't belong here. Get an apartment.

"What do the girls think?" Zar asked. "Why doesn't anybody wanna fuck him?"

"It's his anger," Karma said, tossing her smooth blond mane and flashing Blayz a sneer, safe in the knowledge that her blue wristband trumped his brown one. "He's mad at all of us up front 'cause he's sure we're gonna say no, and who wants that vibe coming at them? It's like he's *asking* us to reject him."

Zar shrugged. "Sounds right to me." Jaw tight, eyes hard, he turned to Blayz. "If you wanna get laid, you better get friendly."

"Fuck," Blayz muttered, and punched the rug. A month later, he and Teal would leave together, around midnight. Zar would escort them off the Farm at gunpoint—supposedly to keep Blayz from stealing a costly camera and tripod. Blayz claimed the equipment was his; he'd brought it with him. Hearing about the standoff the morning after, I would applaud Zar for defending Zendik.

More hands shot up, mine among them. Zar nodded to me. My cheeks burned; my heart pounded. "I haven't had sex in twenty-three years," I said, riffing on Blayz's intro, to a ripple of chuckles. "I'm having a date with Kro tonight, and I'm not fertile. I was wondering if it would be okay for us to have sex."

Zar blinked. Most questions posed at sex meetings resembled Blayz's: saturated with anguish, ignited by pain. Zar squinted into the back of the room. "Is Kro here? What does he think?"

I turned to look where Zar was looking. Kro emerged from the shadows by the stairs, a gleeful-yet-bashful grin on his face.

"I'm into it," he said.

Lying naked with Kro under his quilt, on the thickest patch of grass we could find in the lower field, I realized I did not understand the mechanics of sex.

The one sex scene I'd viewed on-screen, at twelve or thirteen, had only confused me. As the parents of the boy hero

in *Empire of the Sun* coupled beneath coarse blankets on a cot
in a refugee camp, I'd squeezed my eyes shut with each gasp
and shift, to block what I thought was coming: blood, oozing
through wool. I'd been sure that one of the two heaving shapes
was struggling to stab the other.

In college, I'd found my vagina, clitoris, and G-spot with
the help of diagrams in *Our Bodies, Our Selves*. But the book
did not show how male and female limbs intertwined during
intercourse. To fill the blank, some renegade part of my brain
doodled a crude placeholder: two pencils, one atop the other,
the top pencil popping a spring-loaded chip in and out of the
bottom pencil's slot. (Why pencils? Why not?)

Maybe I'd never bothered to learn how sex worked
because I'd assumed the man I was meant for—once he'd found
me—would provide all the guidance I'd need.

Across the creek, the bucks snuffled and grunted. A half
moon lit the field, the ridge, the dim hulk of the bare mountain. A low wind skimmed over us. As on the nights of my first
dates with Kro and Estero, other couples had snapped up the
rustic wooden shacks. And I refused to make this passage in
the trailer or a van.

When Kro climbed on top of me, I was playing the pencil role: legs straight, knees closed. He grinned at my ignorance. "Helen, you have to open your legs. So I can get between
them." I complied, glad the light was low enough to hide the
blush creeping toward my ears, neck, forehead.

"You have to bend them, too. Like this." He gently
crooked my knees and caressed my thighs, still smiling down
on me, the half moon forming a faint halo around his short
Afro. Was he atoning, at thirty-four, for the sins of the drunk,
horny, seventeen-year-old, even as he soothed the heart bruise
of all those criminal hands up my skirt?

When I nodded I was ready, he entered me slowly, eyes
fixed on mine, alert for distress signs. The pain of entry gave

way, not to pleasure but to a sense of being filled. *So this is sex*, I thought. *Hmm. Maybe it improves with practice?*

When Kro rolled off me, satisfied, I felt as if something momentous had happened, then dissolved before I could grasp it. He stretched out on his back and curled his arm around my shoulders. A chill snuck under the quilt. I nestled into his warmth.

Staring up at the southern stars, I silently blessed the Farm for giving me a chance at sweetness—if not ecstasy—in my first experience of sex. For helping me share this crossing with a man who made me feel more myself, not less. In a far-distant time, when other thank-yous to Zendik would strike me as silly and wrong, this one would still sound true.

Sex at Zendik was both upper and opiate. Its spectrum of thrills and burns—attraction, pursuit, orgasm; envy, censure, rejection—quickened the daily plod while dulling the ache of lost freedom. Selling was similar. Just as we "hit up" potential lovers for dates, we "hit up" potential buyers on the street. Coming with a lover was called getting "off"; finding flow as a seller was called getting "on." Selling had its own range of lows and highs, all intertwining with our quest for love, our sense of worth, our standing in the tribe.

I'd learned early on that the Zendiks made almost all their money selling magazines, CDs of their music (Wulf's dirges and tone poems, Arol's laments and protests), and Stop Bitching Start a Revolution bumper stickers at concerts and festivals, and on city streets, all over the Southeast, Midwest, and Northeast. I'd also learned that all of the women—barring Arol, Swan, and a couple others in the Family—went selling regularly, as did many of the men.

At first, I'd shied away from selling. But every weekend I spent at home, with mostly just the new guys for company, strengthened my desire to be out on the road, fusing with my fellow warriors in the crucible of a covert mission discharged in a war zone. (Sellers risked getting their "ammo" confiscated— or, worse, getting arrested—if they failed to "shield" themselves from security guards and police.) *I* wanted to depart the Farm in a rush of excitement and return with thick stacks of cash, sheened in fatigue and victory.

The cash—all the sellers had made, less whatever they'd spent on gas, ice, parking, "treats" from the health-food store, the occasional cheap motel room packed with as many Zendiks as could fit on the beds and floor—went straight to Arol and Swan, who in turn rendered regular offerings to their own implacable masters. What each seller kept for herself was pride in having done well or shame for having done badly.

I went selling for the first time, one Saturday in early December, with Loria and Vera, the curly-haired Kore member whose dinner plans had puzzled me my first night at the Farm. On the quaint, redbrick main street of Athens, Georgia, I watched Vera "hit up" passersby with the magazine and a cry of "Underground art mag!" or "Save the endangered humans!" If they stopped to page through the mag, she'd say, "We get donations for it, two to five dollars," spiel briefly about the Zendik way of life as our sole hope for survival, and then launch her upsell, pulling item after item out of her crammed cargo pocket: "If you throw in five, you get a sticker *and* a mag." "It's ten to fifteen for a mag, a sticker, and a CD." "For twenty, you get a mag, a sticker, and *two* CDs."

After ten or fifteen minutes weighing the agony of delay against the terrifying prospect of seeking money from a stranger, I pounced on a pale wisp of a man who looked as fearful as I felt.

"Hey, have you seen this?" I squeaked, charging in front of him and thrusting the mag in his face. "It's an underground art magazine. We get donations for it. We're a group of sixty artists and we live on a farm in North Carolina and we grow our own food and do all kinds of art and music. We think the world's screwed up and we're starting a revolution to—"

The man jerked his head—in accord? alarm?—thrust two wrinkled singles at me, grabbed the mag, and scurried off.

"Thank you!" I called after him, both taken aback by how quick the exchange had been and elated to have made a sale.

I'd consummated my relationship with selling. I was now a Zendik seller.

I went on to make $106 that day—about $7.50 an hour, if you discounted the round-trip drive to Athens, Zendik's investment in the goods we sold, and time spent on "road prep": cooking and packing food; marshaling ammo; assembling bedding, cookware, water, and other aids to remaining self-contained away from home. Vera and Loria had each topped two hundred—the unofficial border, for a seasoned seller in a decent scene, between pride and shame. I'd done well, for a novice, even if I hadn't gotten "on." I trusted that selling, like sex, would improve with practice.

Up in the Addition, Arol and Swan tracked weekly expenses, made monthly mortgage payments, juggled credit cards, and balanced current cash needs against reserve targets for each selling trip. But I witnessed none of this and heard only the occasional tidbit about the Farm's finances. So I saw my wad of cash not as next week's egg buy, or last month's phone bill, or license to add a toothbrush to the communal shopping list, but as a gauge of my value to Zendik.

Later in December, I joined Karma, Teal, and Riven on a two-day trip to Charleston. By the end of our second late night, I'd lost fear of the elegant, clean-cut drunks swarming out of the bars on Market Street. High on contact and loose with exhaustion, I sold multiple double CDs, broke two hundred for the first time, and inspired Karma to dub me Hellion. (I belonged to the small minority of Zendiks who never succeeded at being rechristened; Hellion would remain only a nickname.) I hadn't "gotten on"—but I *had* come close.

In late January, I was sent with six others on a trip to Fort Lauderdale that would last five days—two in the van, three on the street. Saturday and Sunday, we'd sell the Las Olas Art Fair—a throng of white tents and tanned couples—till early evening. Friday and Saturday nights, we'd sell Riverwalk—a cul-de-sac packed with glitzy bars and clubs—and A1A, our shorthand for a busy strip of boardwalk lining a highway of the same name.

I was pleased that Rayel, Teal, and the others who set the selling schedule had deemed me fit for such a long trip. I hoped to pick up in Fort Lauderdale where I'd left off in Charleston.

I had not reckoned with the peculiar challenges of selling South Florida.

It was understood that Zendik sellers leaned toward hitting up members of the opposite sex—maybe because selling had started, in the late seventies, as a channel for meeting new people and expanding the dating pool. If you were lucky, you might find a hot guy or girl you could go home with—or, better yet, one you could lure to the Farm. (Back then, the magazine—called the *Cosmic Revolutionist*—had been a stapled sheaf of mimeographed pages, selling for a dollar; the group relied largely on busking, shoplifting, and welfare for survival.) Or maybe we were acknowledging that people often gave us money out of appreciation for a personal connection; why not enrich that link with a touch of flirtation? With experience, I would learn to approach couples, men in pairs and groups, women in pairs and groups, and single women. But in the beginning, I hit up mostly single men, zeroing in on the disheveled, disaffected, afraid, and misshapen. If they had dreadlocks or a Mohawk; if they wore chains, tie-dye, leather, or anything marked SLIP-KNOT; if they paired superhero trucker caps with Coke-bottle glasses; if they stank of Nag Champa—so much the better.

They were all the more likely to stop for a woman with no special gift of attraction.

Friday night, plying A1A with Karma and Donna (a longtime seller and Kore member who was also Zar's girlfriend), I watched in envious wonder as they sold magazines, stickers, *even CDs*, to a parade of couples I shrank from approaching. Thin, bronzed women pranced by on the arms of silver-haired gentlemen, silicone breasts bulging out of bikini tops like overripe oranges. The man, I learned, would always spring to his honey's wish or bow to her veto. He might carry the cash and be ready to spend it, but all it took was one curl of a frosted lip, one stomp of a stiletto, to shock his wallet back to his pocket.

Crushed to the point of tears, after dozens of failed hitups, I asked Karma and Donna for help. Karma advised me to go ahead and cry; the only way to get through negative emotions, she said, was to feel them completely. Donna nodded in agreement. "Believe me, I've been where you are. It is *hell*."

I made $17 in about five hours on A1A. In an additional hour or so at Riverwalk, where we joined the four men on our crew, I sold a single bumper sticker, for a single dollar, to the one party person who would give me the time of night: a gangly skateboarder with a jutting larynx and a lazy eye.

On Saturday, teaming with Karma and Donna again, I repeated my plea for help. Karma urged me to try to have fun. "It's all energy! People want what you have when you're having a good time." Selling from about noon till 1:00 or 2:00 a.m., I made $54.

Sunday morning, in the van on the way to Las Olas, I begged to be tutored. "I get that selling's all energy," I said, as we crossed the causeway over glittering Biscayne Bay, "but I just feel like there must be specific techniques you guys could teach me."

Rave—a power seller and Family Apprentice who'd spent five years at the Farm—glanced back at me from the shotgun seat. "I know what you need. Stick with me."

I followed Rave to a spot on Las Olas well past the last of the white tents, where he could train me without provoking Fair security. He advanced to the edge of a hedged plaza in front of a bank (closed, since it was Sunday). I stayed back a few paces. We waited.

An older couple stepped through a break in the hedge and strolled our way. The man sported beige chinos, a cream-colored polo shirt, and a comb-over that could have been stitched from dental floss. The woman wore a toothpaste-blue pantsuit and had dyed-blond hair. Clearly, these were *squares*.

Rave, unfazed, plucked a *We the Poet* CD from his messenger bag, yanked the flap shut, and signaled me to pay attention. Then he bounded toward the couple, flashing a grin big enough to dazzle them both.

"Hey, check out our music!" He handed the woman *We the Poet*. On the cover was Arol in close-up, eyes shut midwail. High contrast and a shimmering overlay had stripped twenty years from her face. "It's supercool rock and roll from our farm near Asheville. Like nothing else you're gonna find down here." He glanced at the man, then back at the woman. "Try it. You'll love it."

They *would*? *We the Poet* was Arol's debut as leader of the Zendik band. Her drummer, bassist, violinist, and guitarists were all skilled musicians, but Arol was a novice singer and lyricist whose improvised vocals skewed toward muddled incantation and shouted rant. Over the years, I would school myself to like her work, and Wulf's: I would listen to their albums on repeat, comply with the tacit requirement that I compliment Arol on each new CD, and impute a Deathculture taint to all other songs. But in the beginning I simply didn't like Zendik music—and wished I did, so I could sell more of it.

As the woman flipped the CD over to scan the list of tracks, Rave whipped out a sticker and mag and pressed them on the man. The mag's newsprint cover showed Swan, nude behind a rippling scrim, caught at the midpoint of a mournful pirouette. Head back, lips parted, eyes shut, she seemed weary of the world's gaze. For years she'd been cast as the starlet whose looks and gifts would sell the public on Zendik.

The man glanced from the mag to the sticker. His lips puckered into a chuckle. Rave blazed on. "As young people, we believe it's our job to work for a better world—to put our ideas into *action*—instead of just whining about how bad things are." He paused to let the man page through the magazine.

I noted the blandness of the language Rave used for his story of Zendik as grassroots Peace Corps. The night before, at Riverwalk, he'd been laying down hard lines, laced liberally with swear words: "We're drowning in bullshit, the oceans are dying, and I'm supposed to take Prozac and get a fucking *job*?" As a final flourish, he liked to clasp a hand to his throat, give a quick, strangled bark, and ask, "What are you gonna do—stock shelves at Kmart while Flipper chokes on plastic bags?" Rave, now twenty-one, had finished high school a year early so he could move to the Farm at sixteen. Later, he'd signed over his $4,000 college fund. He truly believed he was defending a planet in distress. What we Zendiks lost sight of was the vast, many-hued tapestry into which were woven both the black hole of working at Kmart and our own supposed white knighthood.

Rave raked his long, knobby fingers through his short, Norse-blond hair, making shocks of it stick up at crazy angles. "People help us out with donations," he said. "Twelve to twenty for the CD. If you throw in twenty, you get the sticker and the zine."

The man slipped the sticker inside the mag and handed it to the woman. Then he pulled out his wallet and gave Rave a twenty. Rave smiled, thanked them both, and waved as they resumed their stroll.

I was agog. I'd never seen a seller go straight for the big bucks, or so fully take control. Had Rave been born with the superpower of adamant self-confidence? Or was this a Zendik form of sorcery he could pass on to me?

Rave marched my way, pupils dilated with rising excitement. "Your turn, Hellion! Do what I did. Sell me a CD."

I wiggled a mag at him. "Have you seen this?"

"No!" He grabbed the mag out of my hand. "Lead with the CD. And start with a command, not a question. *You're* in charge here. Not them."

I tried again, feigning enthusiasm. "Hey, check out our supercool rock and roll!" Maybe I didn't *have* to like the music, or believe the squares would, to part them from their cash. Rave seemed to be saying he didn't care if they liked it or not. Their role was to support us. By buying our stuff. And *our* role—as I'd heard Arol put it while rallying the troops—was to "shove it down their throats."

Once I'd succeeded at "selling" Rave a CD, he sicced me on a couple in his-and-hers Hawaiian shirts. With him coaching me, in mime, from a few feet behind them, I felt my confidence surge. They bought a $5 mag. The next couple bought a double CD. It was as if Rave had sucked his persuasive power into a needle and shot it into me.

After selling a few more mags and a couple more CDs, I crossed over into the flow known as being "on" and stayed there all afternoon, savoring the intoxicating illusion that I could steer people to buy with my mind. My pants pocket bulged with a swelling wad of bills.

The art fair closed at five. We stuck around to hit up the diehards straggling back to their cars. Into gaps between hit-ups crept dread of the moment when my "on" spell would end. Though I felt power over my buyers, I felt no power over the power itself; I could no more cajole it to stay than I could prolong a date with Estero. I hoped, at least, to get off the street before it evaporated.

Finally, at six, Rave signaled me to quit.

Now we would count.

Crammed in the van together, thumbs sucking up the musk of sweaty ink and cotton, the seven of us wrangled our wads of cash in silence. As I smoothed, faced, and ordered my bills—sleek Jacksons, crisp Hamiltons, wrinkled Lincolns, worn Washingtons—I wondered how my number would compare with the others'. Only Rave and I were in high spirits. There was a chance I'd made more than he had. Could it be that I, once paralyzed by shyness, had come from behind to best everyone?

As a freshman at Dominican Academy, I'd lived for the days when Mrs. Gilleaudeau, our most demanding teacher, handed back biology exams, starting with the lowest grade and climbing to the highest. The prize of bitter admiration, of acid stares at the lockers, went to whoever received her exam back last. I never questioned the competition's premise. I almost always won the prize.

Once my notes were neatly sorted, I counted, counted again to check my math, then passed the stack to Karma, folded in half.

Rave looked up. "How much?"

"One forty-eight."

Karma smiled. "Go, Hellion! Good job!"

"Yeah," said Donna. "You rocked."

Rave wiped the sweat from his forehead. "Whew!" he said, handing over his own stack and grinning at me with a mix of relief and mischief. "One fifty-one. For a second there, I thought you were gonna beat me."

Emboldened by my success on Las Olas, I asked Rayel to send me to Mardi Gras in early March. She laughed. "New Orleans would eat you alive!"

Maybe she believed me when I swore I could brave the challenge. Or maybe Rave convinced her to give me a shot. Either way, I made the list. I'd be one of nineteen Zendiks selling the six-day carnival in two overlapping shifts.

As soon as we arrived in the French Quarter, New Orleans pounced—canines bared, slobber streaming from its mouth. The gutter punks—a loose gang of pierced, tattooed homeless kids with fierce dogs—jeered us and snarled at the sight of our merchandise. (It was they, most Zendiks thought, who had slashed our van tires and siphoned sugar into our gas tanks during previous trips to New Orleans.) A sludge of piss and vomit squelched under my sneakers as I shoved through the crush of drunks on Bourbon Street. (I shouted, "Check out our magazine!" They chanted, "Show your tits!") The truly smashed—I'd heard from other sellers—sometimes fucked and blew each other in dark alleys and doorways. If you didn't watch out, you might find your eyes slimed by real-life porn.

Our punishing schedule made us only more vulnerable. Since the Quarter never emptied, it was usually 2:00 or 3:00 a.m. before we staggered back to the van, counted our cash, and drove to our crash pad, a supporter's one-bedroom apartment. There, sardined on her floor, we grabbed a few hours' fitful sleep, before rising at 7:00 or 8:00 a.m. to prep for a late-morning or early-afternoon return to the Quarter.

In the van, under the bench seat, was a stack of thick black trash bags. At the end of our final night, we would seal inside them our stinking shoes, our sodden pants—anything wet with the spit of New Orleans—pretending we could repel viral invasion by throwing the clothes and shoes in the washing machine and sending the bags to the landfill. But by that time legions of pathogens would already be bivouacked inside us. Mardi Gras was infamous for getting sellers sick.

Soon after returning home, I would develop a severe sore throat, then a cough that hacked on for a month. The girls would absolve Zendik thus: I'd vibed into my illness by being overambitious, by plunging too soon into too harsh a war zone. The toll on our bodies was yet another cost we couldn't count if we were to keep faith in selling as the only way to make a living.

Struggling to suck $200 per shift from the frantic baccha-
nal of the French Quarter, I *was* being consumed. But not by
New Orleans.

Saturday, Sunday, and Monday, two hundred, give or take
a few bucks, was all I could manage. But then, on Fat Tuesday—the last day, when throngs of revelers donned masks and
costumes—the game changed.

Within minutes of hitting the street, I hit up a couple dis-
guised as the Big Bad Wolf and Red Riding Hood. The Wolf
growled something at me through his fanged snout. *What did he
say?* She translated: he wanted both CDs. She reached into her
cleavage, pulled out a twenty, and handed it to me. Each day,
I tucked the first money I made into the tiny pouch hanging
from the necklace I'd received from Arol for my twenty-third
birthday, hoping her power would help it multiply. I'd never
before filled it with a twenty.

After making more than $80 in my first hour, I was
called, around noon, to join eleven other Zendiks in a ring
at the intersection of Rue Royale and Rue St. Peter. The sour
scent of spilled beer wafted up from the asphalt. Cardboard
cups littered the gutters. A frantic eddy of jazz, rock, bluegrass,
and zydeco swirled up St. Peter from a cluster of open-front
bars already raucous on Bourbon Street. Thick ropes of beads in
purple, green, and gold looped almost every neck in the swelling crowd. Within our ring, twelve circle-Zs glittered at twelve
beadless throats.

Across the ring from me, Mar—a Kore member, and one
of our crew leaders—twisted the lid off a small plastic bottle.
She'd bought it at Herbal Imports, a head shop a few doors
down St. Peter. The bottle was filled with oblong gray-green
pills. Active ingredients: guarana, ephedra. Trade name: TurboCharge. She shook a couple pills into her palm and passed
the bottle on.

Zendiks were forbidden pot and hard drugs but allowed

caffeine as a spur to harder work. At least one cooler on every Zendik selling trip held a mason jar or gallon jug of black tea. Maybe Mar figured TurboCharge was fine because it hung off the far end of the caffeine continuum. Or maybe she didn't care where it fell, so long as it raised our totals. Maybe no one at home ever had to know.

I'd never smoked pot or tried any other illegal drug. I'd waited till my twenty-first birthday to take my first drink and had drunk only a handful of times in the couple years since. I'd yet to acquire a taste for coffee, which wasn't available at Zendik anyway. Black tea hadn't helped me sell, the couple times I'd tried it. I had no idea how guarana and ephedra would affect me. But after three grueling selling days, with one more to go, I wasn't about to refuse a boost. I palmed the prescribed two pills and washed them down with a swig of water from the common jug.

The "on" spell that followed exploded my understanding of on-ness. On Las Olas, it had seemed that I could push my targets to do as I pleased. This time, I felt myself immersed with the throngs in a river of sisterly love, where I could reach anyone—couples, packs, women, good-looking men. Here the nos rolled off me, the yeses enveloped me. The current dissolved my warrior stance, leaving my calling voice, my outstretched hand. My tale of life as a gushing adventure, rushing with wonder and magic. The tale that had lured me to New Orleans via Zendik.

But all tales that compel are true at their core, and the core of my high on Fat Tuesday was agape. I would feel it other times, in other places, at Zendik and beyond. I would sense the pulse of all beings. Swell with the joy of communion. Know myself as one drop in a stream of infinite richness.

What role the drug played, I cannot say. Maybe it propped me upright. Maybe it lifted the burden of time, the worry that I'd plummet before the end of the night. Whatever it did, I gave it no credit. I forgot I'd taken it. I believed I'd leaped into Wulf's "Infinite Instant, where dwell the Heart and Meaning of Life." What charge I held, what love I shared, welled from Zendik—the new heart, the true meaning, of *my* life.

I was still high at midnight, when a fleet of police cars roared in to clear the French Quarter with shrieking sirens and a blinding hail of blue light. By then, dozens of Zendik magazines lay scattered in the slime. Many had given us money out of drunken magnanimity, not thirst for our philosophy. But to me, the sodden litter signaled victory. Saturation. You couldn't look anywhere, even down, without seeing Zendik. From here, I imagined, our message would travel to realms beyond our ken. It would spread to all continents. We'd crashed—and swayed—the carnival at the crossroads of the world.

Back at our place to stay, all twelve of us piled onto a mound of pillows and sleeping bags to watch *The Matrix* and revel in our smashing Fat Tuesday crescendo. Most of us had broken four hundred. I'd made four sixty. Both crews together, over six days, had grossed $19,500.

I didn't want to see *The Matrix*. Watching it in a theater the previous September, a month before I'd come to Zendik, I'd been terrified by the kinship I'd felt with the fetuses hooked to the grid. I, too, was trapped—in a war machine wired to suck my eight hours a day, my debt and tax payments, my numbed acquiescence. But by March 2000, the story no longer gripped me. Hadn't I escaped the matrix?

Plus, I disapproved of Zendiks' occasional indulgence in "square" movies—to me, tentacles of the Deathculture. Two years later, when the entire Farm would troop off to a local movie house to see *The Fellowship of the Ring*, I would object and stay home, vainly hoping to enjoy my couple hours alone.

I stayed up till 5:00 a.m. that morning after Mardi Gras, not to see Neo through to freedom, but to savor the warmth of belonging. Wulf rose from the page to whisper in blessing: *Yes, the kingdom of heaven is at hand. It's here on this beautiful earth.*

The next weekend, no one sold. On Saturday afternoon,

word filtered down from the Addition to the Farmhouse—from the purples through the grays to the blues, browns, and greens—that we would celebrate our success with a dinner party.

That evening, released by postselling quarantine from serving and cleanup, I sat kitty-corner from Kro at one of the half-dozen folding tables arrayed on the widest of the terraces climbing to the Addition. We'd picked and shoveled these levels, then walled them with stones hauled by pickup truck from a nearby creek and heaved off the tailgate to be puzzled into place. Soon Arol would muster labor to beautify the hillside with a pergola, and flower gardens she'd design. For now, sprigs of wild violet garnished the tables, draped in bedsheets shading from lavender to midnight. Though I wore only a light dress and jacket and it was still winter, I didn't shiver. Kro's heat, the red wine, pride in my share of our triumph, kept me warm. His grin while we drank grew broader and sweeter. His eyebrows rose in sly peaks. As laughter lilted around us, his hand crept from my knee to my thigh to my waist. The embraces of lover and tribe entwined to hold me in what could have been an infinity sign.

[chapter 5]

Last Glimpse of Sunlight

SITTING WITH MY MOTHER at her kitchen table in Brooklyn, I insisted on delivering my version of what had happened in the five months since I'd left her for Zendik.

I needed her to know she was wrong: I hadn't dropped into a work camp with no use for my talents, and I wasn't going through a phase. Zendik was so much more than a bunch of hippies shitting in the woods and a newsprint booklet she didn't see as art. It was the one place on Earth where, in Wulf's words, "children can really love their parents, boys can really love girls, women can really love men."

She *had* to find Zendik worthy and believe I would stay. Otherwise I might be forced to face my closed bank account, my shrunken horizon, the doubts I'd pounded down about the commitment I'd made.

"I just want you to understand why I'm at Zendik," I said.

I was not on a selling trip. I'd taken the bus to New York alone, for a long weekend, with money my mother had sent me. I'd gone on an "out."

As a young Zendik, I was free to leave the Farm for a few days—or weeks, or months—without backlash. Either I'd succumb to my old story—proving I'd never been battle-worthy—or return to the Farm hot for combat. Older Zendiks, on the other hand, paid for the breaks they took. As tenure lengthened, leaving turned to betrayal.

I'd arranged this out because, in the month since Mardi Gras, I'd lost heart. Gone dull. And stayed that way, despite a litany of stratagems devised to revive myself:

I hiked up the mountain to sing, hoping for a chance to sing with the band.

I got Swan's permission to join her dance class.

I practiced walking on a pair of stilts a carpenter built me.

I did backbends in lull moments and somersaulted down slopes.

I had dates with a few new men, seeking one as attentive as Kro, as charged as Estero.

I strung one hundred lengths of fishing line across the door frame of the little room in the barn loft, to feel the sting of a hundred threads snapping against my legs and chest.

I lay on the floor of the loft with fifty-pound discs on my heart and gut—testing, when I lifted them, for hints of levitation.

I hauled a fifty-pound grain sack up and down the hill from the barn on my shoulders, for the thrill of lightness I felt when I dropped the weight.

I doodled in pebbles on the cave floor while a boulder rolled in to seal it closed.

I traveled to Brooklyn for assurance that love as I desired it did not exist beyond the cave.

If I stood at the kitchen window and squinted, I could see the Statue of Liberty, lifting her lamp above the harbor. Sitting at the table, I faced away from her.

"I never told you this," I continued, glancing from my mother to the jars of beans and grains on the shelves at her shoulder, "but when I was in college, I hooked up with guys I met on the road a couple times, and I felt like I had to keep that stuff secret from just about everyone, especially you."

She held my gaze, chair angled toward me. She'd converted to Catholicism in her forties. Neither her 1950s upbringing nor her adopted religion had equipped her to speak frankly about sex, or even brief me, when I was a teenager, on the apocryphal birds and bees. This was the kind of conversation we didn't have in my family. Yet we were having it.

"At Zendik it's different. Sex is part of life. We all talk about it, right out in the open. No one has to be ashamed or keep secrets. I feel like I can finally show I'm a sexual person." I was tearing up now. "And that's really important to me."

Once, I'd seen my mother kiss my father. Once, I'd surprised them in bed together. Mostly she slept in the guest room and kept to the kitchen and dining room, while he sequestered himself in a large parlor divided by a curtain into sleeping and work spaces. In that apartment—larger than the one she lived in now—a long hall separated her domain from his.

In the summer of 1999—shortly before I moved to Zendik, and seven years after my parents' divorce—my mother asked me to write a statement in support of her request for an annulment from the Catholic Church. Divorce dissolves a union. Annulment decrees it never happened.

In my statement, I set down for the first time an image I'd long associated with my parents' marriage: two ladder shafts, standing parallel, joined by few, if any, rungs.

Maybe, in breaking with my mother's reticence, I hoped to shake her example and gain a chance at loving partnership with a man.

I could tell by the way she pressed her lips together that she was both bewildered by my outburst and working to absorb it. Behind her, morning sun seeped down the hallway from the living room. She pressed her hand, palm down, onto the table.

"You be Jesus," she said. "I'll be John the Baptist. Do what you're called to do. I don't need to know your reasons."

John the Baptist had prepared the way for a messiah, blind to the storm his coming would stir. She would stand behind me through my journey, despite the nightmares it would bring her. She spoke with respect, and surrender.

But my hanging judge heard something else: proof that she was, as charged, too prudish to mother me through womanhood. Arol alone, with her lush mane and young lover, could fill that role.

Soon after I returned to the Farm, I wrote my mother a poem I would not have dreamed of showing her. In it, I divided myself from her, my lovers from her ex-husband: "Listen, mother—/ I am not your daughter/ I am fucked by strong men/ Your man had brittle bones/ A leg of stones/ And no love to give you then." Also, I offered hope. Maybe if *I* could form a loving helix with a man, I could someday guide her past her years in bitter parallel: "Listen, mother—/ I will find another/ Way to be with men/ I'll have less alone inside my bones—/ And love to give you then."

[chapter 6]

Tough Love

SITTING CROSS-LEGGED ON carpet the color of eggshells, my back against the wall, I snuck glances at the other sellers on my crew and let dread build in my chest. Cayta, our leader, had summoned us to the plush living room of our host's swank bachelor pad as soon as he'd left for his Saturday-morning workout. It was August in Chicago. August 2000. A few months had passed since my visit to Brooklyn. As the humidity rose outside, a purring cooling system pumped stale gusts throughout the gleaming high-rise. Air-freshener discs littered the apartment. I mouth-breathed to fend off their scent of orange Starburst.

My crewmates, also on the floor, faced me in a loose half circle. Riven chewed a fingernail. Toba straightened the CDs and magazines in her patchwork shoulder bag. Taridon crossed and uncrossed his outstretched legs, trying to get comfortable without kicking the coffee table. Owen, bony shoulders bent forward, studied a worn copy of "The Affirmative Life." He and I had gone on a couple dates in the past month. On Wednesday night, we'd stayed up late in the kitchen, letting the buzz of flirtation power us through the last few hours of road prep. But I didn't expect him to help me now. He stood no higher than I did on the Zendik pyramid.

Cayta, squarely across from me, locked her eyes on mine. "So. Do you want to take the bus home?"

I squeezed my thumb. My knuckles blenched. I stared at my lap to hide my panic.

I'd heard about taking the bus home.

Back in May, the girl who slept next to me in my new dorm, the Old Music Room, had returned from a blockbuster festival in Memphis via Greyhound. Frenzied with penitence, she struggled through sobs to explain what she'd done to deserve expulsion from her selling crew. Her story was messy and blurry. I couldn't make sense of it. What I did get, all too clearly, was the horror of this form of censure. Those who received it stood one step from exile.

Against my roommate's torrent of shame, I'd thrown up a psychic dike. *That*, I'd thought, *is not going to happen to me.*

But my dike had not repelled the wave of "input"—criticism—that had swelled with each selling trip I'd gone on since Mardi Gras. In Charlotte, the girls on my crew had accused me of riding an "ego jack" over my "apprentice attitude." In Pensacola, I'd had "no push"—I hadn't been "righteous" enough about demanding people's money. In Atlanta, I'd been "a loner," "running my own show." The day before, in Evanston, a suburb north of Chicago, I'd been "competitive" and "unconnectable."

We called it input because, like data added to a map, it was supposed to help us find our evolutionary coordinates and chart a path forward. But really it was ammo in our battle with each other for a share of Arol's favor. We Zendiks were not innately petty or nasty. We were scrambling for belonging in a scheme that made it scarce.

Cayta repeated the question, her voice a steel rail. "Helen. Do you want to take the bus home."

What I really wanted was to ride the elevated train all day, staring out scratchitied panes at trees of heaven shooting up through dying buildings' iron skeletons. Alone with my thoughts. Alone but with others. Still but in motion. A couple years earlier, at home in Brooklyn during my year off from college, I'd quit a dead-end job one morning, then spent the rest of the day riding the F train back and forth from Jamaica to Coney Island, reading E. Annie Proulx's *Accordion Crimes* and letting a mind beyond words mull what came next.

"No," I said. "No, I don't. But I feel like maybe if I could go off on my own for the day, I'd be ready to come back tomorrow—"

Cayta cut me off. "*What?* You wanna hang out, do whatever, *in a war zone?*" She leaned toward me, eyes molten. "We don't have time for that. It's either sell or take the bus home. You decide. Now. I'll give you sixty seconds."

She didn't have a stopwatch. It didn't matter. She'd yell, "Cut!" when she chose.

Riven and Taridon nodded. Toba stared past me, down the hall. Owen shoved "The Affirmative Life" into his back pocket, then straightened his back and folded his legs into lotus. Was he soothing a sympathetic panic? Warding off my chaos?

My mind lurched for a thought and went sprawling. Knocked flat by the surge of *no time*.

My gut, sensing a tsunami on the way, grabbed Cayta's looped rope.

"I want to sell!" I said, my plea breached by sobs I couldn't stop. "I wanna go out today and do better."

I didn't want to do better. I wanted my power. What passed as tears of penance were really tears of rage.

A month later, back at the Farm, on a weekday morning, I watched from our own familiar living room floor as a dozen Family members filed in from the kitchen and filled the couch and chairs we'd left clear for them: Zar first, then Rayel, Swan, Prophet, and the rest. I breathed deeply, savoring the cinnamon-citrus scent of ripening persimmons. A thrill quivered in my throat. Impromptu meetings like this usually signaled a big shift.

I happened to know what had triggered the meeting. I'd been up in the Addition the previous afternoon, discussing the dinner plan with Shure, when I'd overheard Arol ask Zar and a few others why the vibe on the Farm had been so heavy lately. Though I hadn't sensed the weight myself, I trusted she was onto something. *What could it be?* Hovering in the office doorway, heart pounding, I risked a guess—which Arol received with a nod and a smile. But she wasn't in the room now. Up the hill with the kids, she'd left Zar in charge.

The late-September sun blazing through the picture window made his pale hair a halo. Knees thrust wide, he leaned forward. "Okay," he said, "let's get this over with. There's a lotta bitching around here about 'Zendik isn't doing it right.' It's time to clear that shit out. We're never gonna win this revolution if we're divided in the ranks." He clenched his jaw. The groove of the knife scar on his right cheek deepened. "What we're gonna do here is we're gonna go around the room and everybody's gonna say their complaints, so we can get them out and get on with it."

The thrill in my throat fanned out through my chest. Zar's pitch fit a pattern I'd first perceived ten years earlier through William Blake's poem "A Poison Tree": "I was angry with my friend;/ I told my wrath, my wrath did end./ I was angry with my foe:/ I told it not, my wrath did grow." Before Zendik, I'd found that sharing wrath with those I cared about could clear our sphere for warmth. At Zendik, I'd seen that wrath mimicked gravity: it flowed *down* the pyramid, only. This was my chance to let loose at least a trickle of the rage I'd dammed in Chicago.

As Zar spoke, Rayel ducked away from her spot up front to hand me a pen and a spiral notebook. In a whisper, she asked if I'd write down what people said. I nodded, eager to be of service. She returned to the couch.

Zar jabbed his chin at Estero, standing by the kitchen door. "You first."

Estero admitted he'd always doubted a revolution could succeed without violence. Rook, another Kore member, said he had a hard time believing a woman could lead the world. Luya said she felt frustrated by her lack of access to Arol: the Family acted like a phalanx of vice presidents keeping her from the chief executive. Out of about forty-five lower-level Zendiks, only two—Kro and Toba, speaking from a dim back corner—claimed no complaint.

"I feel like my life is finally set up so I can go," Kro said. "Like I'm ready to reach my potential."

Toba nodded. "I feel the same way."

Maybe Arol had recently commissioned Kro to write the Wulf section of the Zendik website; maybe she'd just given Toba full charge of the kids' education. Or maybe not. In my memory, a stone cloud of stoicism weights the air around them. Maybe—having spent more time in Zendik's orbit than the rest of us—they knew better how this would end.

When my turn came, I repeated my plea to Arol from a day earlier: How were we to create a new culture, with no time set aside for reading, writing, brainstorming, art making—for shaping it first in our imaginations? I snatched moments for such things from the crush of constant demand.

Then, wanting to stretch this rare chance at comment, I added something I hadn't told Arol: I wished I had an overview of the Farm's workings, a sense of the design guiding our outlays of energy and time. Without that, I felt like a serf, trudging along behind decisions made in the Addition.

Once we'd all spoken, Rayel retrieved my notes. The Family filed out the back door and up the hill to see Arol. The room erupted into happy chatter. I, for one, anticipated praise for my insights. Better yet, I saw all our thoughts swarming to form a new order. What if we collaborated to chart our common course? What if we turned the Addition office into open space for sharing plans and visions? What if we parlayed our freedom from the nine-to-five grind into joyful rhythms of fulfilling work and renewing play?

We were poised for a great leap. I could feel it.

When the Family returned, Rayel was in the lead. Nervous perspiration plastered hanks of dark hair to her forehead. She took Zar's place before the picture window. Standing, not sitting. When she turned to face us, she looked torn between killing and crying.

The room fell silent.

"We were up in the Addition, talking to Arol," she said, "and I realized I had to come back down here and tell you how this meeting made me feel." She bit her lip and cut the tremor from her voice with a sharp breath. "I moved to Zendik Farm when I was eighteen. I've lived here for thirteen years. I'm giving my life to this revolution. And it pisses me off to hear you guys shitting on all the work Wulf and Arol and the rest of us have done to make this incredible place for you to be." Her eyes glittered with outrage now. The threat of tears had passed. "If that's how you feel about Zendik, then you should get out."

Rayel retreated into the line of Family. One by one, those standing with her echoed her anger.

I felt as if I'd unwittingly tripped the latch on a trap door in a hot-air-balloon basket. One moment I was soaring above treetops, seeing farther than I'd ever seen; the next I was flat on my face in a bramble, my world curtailed to the anguish of thorns.

So long as the Family was haranguing us all, as a group, I could handle the anguish. Yes, I'd transgressed. But, with just two exceptions, so had everyone else. Retribution borne by a group could pierce only so deep.

I'd forgotten the notes I'd taken, at Rayel's request.

Moments after the Family had finished, Arol appeared in the kitchen doorway.

Outside, a dog barked. Car tires crunched on the gravel drive. A visitor? A neighbor? No one moved.

Her upper lip twitched, then curled into a sneer that bared her canines. She shook her head. "When these guys showed me the complaints you guys were making, I was *shocked*. We feed you and clothe you and give you this beautiful home and this lifesaving philosophy, and in return you bitch about these *nit*picky little things."

The sneer crept from her mouth to her eyes, which locked on Luya's. "You. You think Swan and the rest of them are keeping you away from me? Maybe if you pulled your head out of your box and quit mooning over what's-his-name, you'd come up with something I'd wanna hear. And you," she snarled, whipping to Rook. "You think a woman can't run Ecolibrium? Who do you think runs this *farm*? Who do you think was keeping it together, even *before* Wulf died?"

One by one, she skewered everyone who'd done as Zar had asked.

When she turned to me, my bladder clenched in dread. Still, I met her eyes. "Weren't you up in the Addition—*where all the decisions get made*—just *yesterday*? You want rules, classes, worksheets. You want someone to set things up so they're just right. Well, get over it. This ain't college. Here, *you* make your life happen."

Thinking she was finished, I dropped my eyes to my lap. I was wrong. She had one more spine to drive in. "But no. You're too good for that. You're always hanging back, judging—*taking notes*—instead of throwing in. Getting real. I'm sick of your snotty, superior, intellectual bullshit."

She moved to her next mark. I shrank inward, cheeks

burning. *If only I'd kept my mouth shut,* I thought. *If only I'd known those were stupid, petty things to say.*

When Arol had finished, Swan, standing at her shoulder, took over. "It seems like people have a lot of resentment about the levels. Like you guys blame Mom and the Family for your lives not being perfect." She paused. Her accusation drifted out into the room and settled on us, like soot. "So from now on there are no levels. It's up to everyone, equally, to make this revolution happen." Her nostrils flared. Her rib cage rose. Her eyes narrowed in challenge. "From now on you're either a Zendik or you're not. Step up or leave. Right now. I want a show of hands. Raise your hand if you want to be a Zendik. If you don't *really* want it, don't raise your hand. We need a core that's committed, not a crowd of hangers-on."

Ten years earlier, in an interview for the Zendik magazine, Swan, age fourteen, had said, "There's some people that are never going to learn to become Honest, and those are the people we call Incorrigibles. And that's sad 'cause they can't *ever* be really happy." A year later, in another interview, she'd been asked "how anybody might go about . . . being honest all the time." She'd replied, "Join Zendik Farm."

Swan had grown up in a stockade made of stories. Inside dwelt truth and the possibility of pleasure. Outside lurked lying and pain.

Raise your hand if you want to be a Zendik. In my eleven months at the Farm, I'd built my own fortress—not as strong as Swan's, but strong enough. *What if I* don't *raise my hand?* I'd be out on the highway by nightfall, adrift in a hell of cloaked figures whose lips, unbidden, twisted thoughts into lies.

What if I do *raise my hand and I'm lying?* Could I muster the depth of allegiance Swan demanded? *Should I or shouldn't I? How will I know?*

I snuck glances at Owen, Rebel, and two other men who'd worn green with me and now, as I did, wore brown.

Owen raised his hand. The other three raised theirs.

I was *at least* as committed as they were.

Within one fraught minute, every hand was raised.

As the meeting broke up, I told myself we *had* advanced toward *égalité*, just not by the path I'd imagined. Maybe we'd find hive mind along a trail of snipped wristbands. But in my body I felt no burst from the Bastille. I huddled in my cell, still, awaiting communion.

In an essay that would eventually appear in the Zendik magazine, I cast Zendik's harshness as a mark of nobility, and my desire for its regard as one I could satisfy by working harder: "I was not born a Zendik; I chose to become one. There is no illusion here of unconditional love. No bond not dissoluble, in a culture based on survival. None but the ones you choose to commit to." I failed to note that commitments made to Zendik were not reciprocated.

I could have been a battered woman, defending her man: He hits me because I've done wrong. I deserve his blows. He knows what I need better than I do; pain helps me grow.

The longer I spent at Zendik, the surer I grew that corruption lurked in my core, like a deeply rooted plantar wart. I *had* to gouge it out—even if my surgeon's kit comprised only scissors and a safety pin.

Dymion had been at the Farm for almost eighteen years. He'd worn a purple wristband before the meeting that had healed so little and hurt so much. At thirty-nine (to my twenty-four), he was lean and muscular. He ran, lifted weights, and played bass with Arol in the Zendik band. Only a receding hairline betrayed his age.

When Dymion had moved to the Farm, in the early eighties, drug use and shoplifting had both been common. Stories

I heard about this time seeded images of roles he might have played before I arrived:

A man crouches in a curtained room and pulls a shoebox out from under a low, homemade, plywood bed. From a neat array of pills, powders, and paraphernalia, he selects a few items. He doesn't rush, though the door might open at any moment. Everyone knows he's the Farm's source for drugs.

A man stands in the produce aisle of a supermarket, harshly lit by overhead fluorescence. He wears a tentlike black trench coat, lined with satchel-size pockets. Shifting a concealed maple syrup jug so it won't poke his ribs, he pretends to inspect the lettuce.

What strikes me now about these vignettes is the lack of malice or calculation in the man's face. He's a dealer, a thief—where's the curled lip, the chill squint? In scenes both real and conjured, I see the same kind eyes behind round lenses, the same raised brows, the same faint grin. I see a man swept along, surprised but willing.

It was this man I enlisted, in February 2001, to help me enact a rape fantasy.

Whose rape fantasy?

Mine?

Or Zendik's?

Before Zendik, I'd imagined being guided through sex by a man who knew, without asking, precisely how to pleasure me. I see now this scenario involved neither attack nor indifference: How could a man bring me to bliss without learning me intimately?

But when Cayta had charged me with attracting sexual violence, I hadn't fought back. Further, I'd adopted the Zendik conviction that the first step in cleansing a Deathculture taint was digging all the way into it. And I'd read a play by Wulf, *The Oraculum Interrogations*, in which a character named Girl, hitchhiking cross-country, is raped repeatedly by a pair of truck drivers. She is puzzled because she loves it. (Cayta would later suggest that I audition for the role of Girl, in a never-completed film version of the play. I would demur and be cast as an entranced soothsayer instead.)

Rather than depict the rape of Girl in sensual detail—which would have required him to show how a woman might be aroused by force, without foreplay—Wulf had her describe it afterward, in the language of pleasure, thereby claiming that rape and rapture belong together.

As a young Zendik who'd been having sex for less than a year—and had never had sex beyond Zendik—I was primed to believe Wulf's claim. I didn't know my sexual self well enough to ask how I could expect to reach orgasm without so much as a chance to get wet.

Maybe I credited Dymion with magical powers. He *did* live in the Addition—where, I imagined, sexual prowess seeped through your skin while you slept. The first date we'd gone on, in late January 2001, had been my first with an erstwhile member of the Family.

At that moment, we'd matched: I was still aching for Owen, in the wake of a split forced by Swan's condemnation of our relationship during a full-group meeting. Dymion, under duress, had recently made a final break with his on-again, off-again girlfriend of the past few years. Had we been left to our other loves, I would not have sought him out. He would not have heard my call.

Dymion had been at Zendik long enough not to be fazed by strange sexual propositions. He was used to the idea of the date space as laboratory for therapeutic experiment. Shure was, too. So when I asked her to hit Dymion up for a date—our third—involving simulated rape, she did not try to dissuade me. Nor did she mention that he—alone among the handful of Zendiks with herpes—was known to manifest instant outbreaks during dates that made him nervous. (Those who had herpes could get together with those who didn't, so long as they showed no symptoms that day. Usually sores bloomed slowly.) She nodded, shrugged, agreed.

Dymion, it turned out, had played the rapist before. After accepting my request through Shure, he approached me in person to tell me this and convey his excitement. Years earlier, in Texas, when he and Toba had been together, they'd tried something similar: She'd gone for a run on a deserted road. He'd pulled her into the woods and mock-raped her. They'd both enjoyed the transgressive story line. They'd been lovers for a few years by then.

The night of our date, I dressed up in a newish pair of blue jeans and a royal-purple button-down shirt. I was sitting cross-legged on the double bed in the date space by the Old Music Room when Dymion arrived. He stood facing me, filling the narrow strip of floor separating bed from door. He wore tight black jeans and a thin, sleeveless shirt, unbuttoned to show his hard pecs and taut stomach. A fat candle in a dusty dish flickered on the night table, next to a roll of toilet paper. I imagine the candle casting a dull glow over a smudged copy of *The Psychic Compass* (Zendik's answer to the *I Ching* or tarot), opened to the oracle I seemed to choose with unusual frequency: "Your Lie Equals Your Pain."

"So, how should we do this?" he asked. "We could role-play—I'm the lecherous teacher, you're the innocent schoolgirl."

I'd yet to accept that stories turn me on, that I'm likely to get wetter when staging erotic dramas in my head. I'd heard Arol ream other Zendiks for being "in fantasy" during sex. It was disrespectful to your partner, she'd said—a hedge against intimacy. Anyhow, what Dymion was suggesting sounded more like seduction than rape.

"No, I don't wanna role-play. I just wanna do it. You come at me, I'll fight, you overpower me and fuck me anyway."

"Okay."

He threw me down on the bed. I lay back, looking up at him. He ripped the buttons off my shirt, ripping it open. I pushed against his chest—playing my part, even as I began to sense that speed, the speed of force, was the enemy. No heat, no wetness, rose between my legs.

He grabbed my wrists, pressed my arms against the bed. Undid the button at my waist, unzipped my pants, yanked them down.

There was still time. I could have screamed. I could have pushed back again, I could have said, "Look, I know I was supposed to pretend to resist. But I'm not acting now. Stop." I think he would have listened. I think he would have quit.

He unzipped his own jeans, shoved them down enough to free his cock. It was hard. He closed his eyes and forced it into my dry vagina. I flinched in pain. I clenched my teeth. Each thrust felt like a fresh sprawl against asphalt, a fresh scrape to flesh—except this was not the flesh of a knee, but the flesh inside me.

Even then—I could have stopped him. I could have shrieked and clawed.

Why didn't I?

Because something burned more than the sting in my groin: my need to complete the ritual. Cauterize my desire for violence. Force this weakness I'd been charged with to leave my body.

I lay still, aflame with pain. I ached for him to come, so it would end.

For me, the trance—the story of arousal by force—had broken with Dymion's first thrust. For him, it lasted till he withdrew his cock and saw that it was raw and bloody. I was bleeding, too, from a rip in my perineum.

He stood up, stunned. "It hurt a lot," I said. "I didn't expect that. But I didn't wanna stop."

He shook his head, eyebrows peaked in shock. "I had no

idea. I was just playing my part, and now . . ." He gestured at his cock. It was sprouting red droplets. I grabbed the roll of toilet paper and tore off a few sheets to swab my rip. His eyes followed my hand.

"I can't believe I did that," he said.

The next morning I showed Shure the rip, plus the mysterious bump inside my labia that burned when I peed. She gave me ointment to dab on the rip. The bump? That was herpes. Too late, she disclosed Dymion's reputation for flash outbreaks. I was too drained to blame her. Then again—was there blame to be laid? Would disclosure have dissuaded me? Had the sores even figured in transmission of the virus? No one had known we'd both bleed.

Ordinarily we girls were eager for the details of each other's sexual experiences, especially when we sniffed date-space disaster. Debacles made great stories—and only constant vigilance could keep the tinder of our corrupt sexuality from setting the Farm aflame. But this time no one showed interest in hearing what had happened or seeking what it meant.

Had the rape date served its purpose? Vaporized my rape fantasy? I was too battered to answer. Instead, I went quiet. I wrapped myself in my own arms, knowing this was the only holding I would get.

I didn't see Dymion the day after. He departed at dawn to go selling in Athens. I learned of his reaction from Zylem.

Sometime in the afternoon, Dymion called Zylem from the street, plagued by guilt. Zylem knew that Dymion, like me, had been raised Catholic. He also knew that, for the good of the Farm, Dymion needed to forget the date and focus on moneymaking. So Zylem said, half-joking, "Pretend I'm the pope. I absolve you."

A couple years later, after Dymion had left Zendik, I would happen to answer the phone when he called from his new home, in Hawaii. He would apologize for his role in the rape date; I would accept his apology and let it touch me. Eventually I would acknowledge how I'd harmed him by asking him to hurt me.

Yet we had not acted alone. Wulf had been there in the date space, chuckling as we performed a version of the Girl tale. And Arol had been there, ensconced in her director's chair, goading us to twist our simple hope for simple love into something dark and bloody. Watching us betray ourselves to serve the Zendik story.

[chapter 7]

Traitors' Hearts

"I WANT YOU TO BREATHE deeply, relax, let your worries go. Okay?"

Amory, my boyfriend of four months, was standing behind me, his hands on my head. As I inhaled, blood swelled the twin nodes of wasp venom under his palms. I'd just been stung, twice, while sitting on the porch swing. With my exhale, the pain eased a trace. I shifted my tailbone off the lip of the five-gallon bucket he'd turned upside-down for me to sit on. Through the bathroom door roared a tide of voices, as the Farmhouse living room filled for dinner. Steel forks clanked against steel bowls.

By May 2002, the shower line had migrated to the Bathhouse. Still, I worried that someone might barge in and mistake our Reiki session for an illicit date. When else did two Zendiks get to spend time together, in private, behind closed doors?

I shut my eyes and let Amory's warm touch coax the scorch out. I'd been told stings were linked to anger. What was I mad about? Had I gotten pissed at Riven for saying I should do more road prep? Had angry thoughts drawn the wasps to sting me on my head? My shoulders tensed. I needed an answer to the question I expected to hear, the moment the door opened: "Why do you think you got stung?"

Amory added a gentle pulse to his touch. "Just relax, okay? Keep breathing. The more you let your energy flow, the more I can use it for healing."

A few weeks earlier, during a rare Sunday afternoon soccer game, the ball had hit me in the face. Amory had joined me on the grass and rested a reassuring hand on my back. He hadn't asked, "How'd you vibe into that?" The previous afternoon, Riven, flanked by Eile and Karma, had skewered me for not volunteering to help them prep for their upcoming selling trip. He'd given me a hug and offered to help. He hadn't said, "Looks like you'd better get to work on your competitive philosophy."

I deeply appreciated Amory's kindness, his unconditional acceptance. I also feared it. Over and over, I'd heard Arol and others blame offenses such as poor selling performance on couples' "square" behavior. I'd seen lovers leave, both alone and in pairs, under the pall of Arol's belief that devotion between intimates turned them against Zendik. I'd come to understand sexual attraction as a force that threatened both my place in my tribe and my tribe's survival. According to Wulf, "A good friend nails you quickly." Amory didn't nail me at all. I linked my love for him to a recent incident that had almost pushed me off the Farm.

On a late-March trip to Charleston, Riven had confiscated my ammo, saying I was so "negative" she didn't want me around. Later, after begging forgiveness, I'd called home. Amory had answered. I took this as a sign that I'd gone soft on the street because he was too good to me.

Back home, loath to betray others as I'd supposedly betrayed Riven, I asked my peers for a break from selling. They refused. When my name appeared on the selling schedule for the next weekend, I realized that my only escape was to leave the Farm.

Midmorning on the last Friday in March, as the van I was supposed to be in departed for Columbia, South Carolina, I sat alone in the Farmhouse office and called an old boss, hoping he'd rehire me as a cook at the Idaho resort where I'd spent a couple summers during college. No answer. The number didn't work.

Plan B was to call my brother, who lived in Boise. As I moved to lift the receiver, the phone rang. It was Arol, calling down from the Addition. For me.

"I heard you were thinking about leaving," she said.

"Yeah, I'm thinking about it."

"Is it the selling? Do you need a break? Do you wanna stay home for a couple months?"

Relief seeped like honey through my body. *How did she know exactly what I need? Can she read my mind?* Now I knew why Tarrow, who'd known Arol for over twenty years, had once told me that her greatest gift was saving people's lives. I failed to consider that she had ears everywhere. Or that I could easily have acted on my own desire for a breather, had I had the power.

"Yes! I would *love* a break! Thank you *so* much." I would have hugged her, I would have kissed her on each translucent cheek, had she been in front of me.

"All right, then," she said, and hung up.

Staying home meant I'd get to spend more time with Amory. It also meant I'd have to be doubly careful: I was sure to betray Zendik again if I let complacency creep into me with his sweet regard, his healing touch.

Amory rested his left arm on the sill of the van's open window and steered with his right, his bicep bulging ever so slightly as he rounded the curves on Lake Adger Road. The late-morning sun brightened his skin. A contented smile played over his lips. A cool breeze teased the fuzz on his forearms, his cloud of brown hair.

A week had passed since he'd laid his hands on my head. The bumps of the wasp stings were gone.

From the passenger seat, I felt the down on my own arms prickle with the memory of his skin against mine in the date space the previous night. In a flash I imagined the van careening off the next sheer embankment. *Focus on the mission, Helen.* Being off the Farm alone with Amory, in a vehicle, was dangerous enough. I couldn't risk dwelling on my attraction to him or slipping into fantasy.

Really, we were on a routine errand. A couple times a week, a pair of Zendiks made the short drive to Silver Creek and Highway 9 to meet the trucks that delivered most of our groceries. This time, since no other drivers had been available, I'd agreed to go with Amory. I welcomed the chance to spend a half hour alone with him in the middle of the day but worried we weren't evolved enough to keep our vibes pure in square territory.

I glanced over my shoulder to check on our cargo, then turned to Amory, keen to funnel my tension into speakable form.

"You think you'll be able to back the van up to the walk-in? With that big crew working on the brick path, you might not have enough room."

Amory's faint smile widened into a grin. "Relax! Don't worry so much." Taking the wheel with his left hand for a moment, he reached over to touch my wrist in reassurance.

"Did I ever tell you about how I used to drive trucks onto airplanes when I was in the army?"

"No." All I knew about Amory's five-year enlistment was that he'd spent time in Germany and that he'd purposely failed a drug test, by smoking pot, to get himself discharged. My own pre-Zendik past, once a lush wood I freely explored, now stood, gray with mist, behind a high, spiked, wrought-iron fence with no entrance. The only safe stories about life before the Farm were those showing the hero or heroine hitting dead ends in the Deathculture, then resurrecting at Zendik. All other plotlines led to psychic jungles sure to swallow me up. Still, I wanted to hear about Amory driving trucks.

"When my unit deployed to Saudi Arabia for Desert Storm, we had to pack trucks with equipment and drive them onto planes. There's no extra space on a plane. Every square inch counts. And we had to make it so that when we landed we could drive right off. So I was backing these huge vehicles up a ramp into this tight space where I'd be screwed if I didn't get it right."

I imagined Amory at the wheel of a truck, eyes on his side mirror, easing the load behind him into just the right spot. He was the same Amory I knew (no crew cut, no uniform), but sexier than ever, as master of a few hundred horsepower.

"How'd you do? Did you always make it?"

"I might have nicked a mirror once or twice. But yeah, I always made it."

"Wow," I said, wishing we could escape to the date space right then.

He glanced at me and laughed. "So you can see why I'm not worried about backing the van up to the walk-in."

I smiled back, pretending for a moment that we were a square couple on a road trip to the Smokies, with a cargo of coolers and camping gear. That we were free to care for each other in our moving cocoon—free to eat, sleep, detour as we pleased.

We turned from Lake Adger onto Regan Jackson. I dissolved my dream as we neared our driveway—sad to see it fade, afraid it would cost me.

Arol stopped a few feet from my seat on the Farmhouse porch and fixed me in her gaze, jabbing the air with a butter-colored folder.

"It's all shit," she said.

It was midmorning on a day in late May threatening highs in the nineties. Two weeks had passed since my van trip with

Amory. The morning glories climbing the fence at Arol's hip had already wilted in the heat. She slapped the folder against her thigh.

"Don't *ever* sacrifice your art for a guy."

Arol was interrupting the prep meeting for my first selling trip since Charleston. Knowing I couldn't stay home forever, and fearing I'd lose my Warrior edge if I didn't hone it in combat, I'd asked to join the all-girl crew set to sell the Chicago Blues Festival. Now I feared sabotage by my shadow: How could I keep myself from further acts of treason?

I'd already volunteered for more than my share of road prep, bearing in mind the "Affirmative Life" quote "Only in Giving is there Living." I'd listened intently to the other sellers' stories of previous Blues Fests, their tips for dodging security. I'd vowed to do whatever it took to subdue my darker forces before the van pulled out of the driveway the following morning.

"All shit"? What's she talking about? Then I remembered: A week earlier, I'd given Arol a batch of writing from the past couple months. I'd been doing this intermittently for the past couple years.

Most of my pieces were short, since I wrote late at night or in snatches grabbed from communal life. Also, they were stunted: While penning sweeping laments for souls damned to the Deathculture and soaring paeans to an Ecolibrium future, I strung high-voltage wires around the shrunken range within which *I* was allowed to feel and ask. When doubt and rage prowled my fence line, jolts of self-reproach shocked them back.

Once, Arol had liked a batch of poems enough to stage a lunchtime reading. Twice, she'd published personal essays of mine—starring the Farm as savior—in the Zendik magazine. I'd hoped this latest sheaf of poems and stories would evince a breakthrough redeeming my two months at home. I'd even fantasized that Arol, awestruck, would draw me aside to say, "Helen, forget selling. You're the Zendik scribe. *That's* where your genius lies."

Instead, she'd dismissed my work as "shit."

"It's got no heart," she continued. "No guts. It's like you're spinning your wheels, off in la-la land. Why? Because you're all wrapped up in what's-his-name." She snorted, eyes rolling skyward. "Once you're in 'love,' you let everything else fly right out the window."

I nodded, at once relieved that she'd voiced my worst fear and jarred by her scorn for my love affair. Surely she knew what I needed to do to keep it from wrecking my selling.

"Come up to the Addition after lunch," she said. "We'll go over what you wrote."

That afternoon, across from Arol at her glossy kitchen table, in one of four matching chairs, I breathed in the beauty and calm of the best appointed and least chaotic room on the Farm. It did not ring with the din of a dozen conversations. It did not stink of sour milk, cat tiddle, buck musk. It did not collect towels, tools, jars, jackets, shoes. Not one forgotten object defiled its dark and gleaming counters, where clouds of royal blue and midnight, veined in black and silver, massed to form an imperial storm.

High on one wall, an epic collage juxtaposed photos of Arol, Wulf, Swan, and the Farm with illustrations from back issues of the Zendik magazine. The drawing that caught my eye showed the head of a mountain goat, divided into halves: one in solid ink, one in dotted outline. It was captioned "Tomorrow's Ghost" and titled *Extinction*.

From my lap I pulled a half-filled page—a printout of a piece Arol hadn't seen yet. I was hoping she would like it and hear the plea beneath the words for a spiritual cure. She signaled me to begin. Taut with anticipation, I read her the poem.

It began: "I feel DEAD. Just chalk in my throat and cover my eyes and dull out the days as dull they go by." It ended: "PASSION, cold passion, hot ice on my heart, burning and freezing and breaking apart, I need a new heart."

Arol nodded. "*That* one's emotionally honest. That's how you really feel about your nowhere relationship."

I flinched. She'd narrowed the question so quickly. Yes, the deadness I'd described had fed off my dread that the sheltering love I'd built with Amory would soon be condemned. Yes, I could twist this link to mean that loving him had dulled me. But wasn't there more to the story? An additional thread or three? Hints at how lasting love, service to Zendik, and joyous work could interweave? A subtle pattern that Arol, with her genius for lifesaving, was uniquely suited to see?

"You know," she continued, "if it's hard for you to break up with him, you can just put it all on yourself. Make it all about you. Say, 'This isn't working for me. I need some time off.' Or however you wanna phrase it. Don't accuse him of doing anything wrong, don't say it's his fault. That way, he can't argue."

Though rote to most people, Arol's advice was new to me. I'd yet to play the initiating role in a breakup. Now, with Blues Fest looming and no reprieve forthcoming, I saw that to placate Zendik I'd have to dump Amory.

That evening, I called him down to the Farmhouse office from the upstairs room—now our library—where I'd once had my bat cave. In the glow of the bulb at the foot of the steps, I improvised on Arol's script: "Amory, I'm sorry, but I need to take a break from our relationship. With everything I'm going through right now, I could use some space to get my head straight."

He blinked, and stepped back as if I'd hit him. He ran both hands through his cushion of hair, then let them drop to his sides and clench into fists. The same hands that weeks earlier had calmed my wasp stings.

"Does that mean we can't have dates anymore?"

"Yes," I said, beyond entreaty. I'd cauterized my own heart-wound hours before.

He moved to hug me.

I moved away.

To my relief, I sold well at Blues Fest. Then, a few weeks later, I pulled off the rare feat of making $300 in Asheville on a Friday when no special event swelled the modest flow of foot traffic.

Yet my triumphs felt hollow. Riding home to the Farm, I had no warm embrace to look forward to. Worse, I had no faith I would find one. The only compass I knew had steered me to Amory. It seemed that my heart had betrayed me.

Into the ruin of our love crept a desire I feared but couldn't dispel: to revisit the Sawtooths.

The Sawtooth range, rising from the Salmon River valley in southeastern Idaho, was the most beautiful place I'd ever been. During college, I'd spent a couple summers cooking and washing dishes at Redfish Lake Lodge, a resort at the edge of the Sawtooth Wilderness. On days off, I'd set out in search of awe: I knew nothing more sublime than gaining a saddle between two ridges and catching my first glimpse of a glacier lake, shimmering like an emerald in a colossal necklace, down the other side.

As June turned to July, my desire crystallized: I wished to sit at the rim of a crater and gaze into Sawtooth Lake—the deepest, the most serene, of all those limpid pools.

Maybe, reeling from Arol's twin strikes against my match and my writing, I sought appeal to a quieter higher power—one who would not rush to judgment.

Admitting I wished to travel meant risking another betrayal.

When I'd left the Farm to see my mother in Brooklyn, in spring 2000, I'd been an infant Zendik—free to weigh my old life against my new one, sure to be welcomed back once I reached the right conclusion. But by summer 2002, when the Sawtooths began calling, my window for a no-fault "out" had long since closed. I was too old, in Zendik years, to dabble in the Deathculture. Should I choose to take a trip, I'd face immediate confinement behind an etheric electric fence.

I knew this because, in my two and two-thirds years at the Farm, I'd witnessed the exits of more than two dozen

Zendiks. Teal, Zeta, Blayz, Estero, Lyrik, Jayd, Loria, Rebel, Owen, and Dymion were among the departed.

Some left meekly, swearing fealty. Some bristled in defiance. Some glittered with reckless flecks of nothing left to lose.

I wasn't nasty to Zendiks on their way out. From most I kept my distance; a few I hugged goodbye. Always, I caught the scent of living death. Always, I saw a noose close, a neck snap, a heart stop—leaving behind a zombie marionette. I felt *certain*, after Zeta left the Farm, that she would never laugh again.

Still. I had to see the Sawtooths.

I called my brother in Idaho and told him I'd leave the next day—July 10. I couldn't set an arrival date, since I didn't yet know how I'd cover the 2,250 miles between the Farm and Boise. I planned to be gone two weeks.

Tarrow—who'd never risked an "out" herself—suggested I take a pretend journey instead. "Can't you stay home and play out the fantasy in your imagination?"

Rave, ever the optimist, insisted I had an eminently curable self-esteem deficit. "You do great selling, and then—bam!—you lose it again. You have to *believe* in yourself, Helen!"

Riven dismissed the news with a weary shrug. "It takes work to survive, wherever you are. I guess if you want, you can learn that the hard way."

That night, after dinner, I retreated to my latest dorm, the Potato Shed, to prepare for my trip. I'd have to trim my needs to fit my medium-size backpack, stow any loose belongings under my bed in banana boxes, and wrestle the bulky sleeping bag I'd found in the barn into a bedroll I could strap to my pack.

My bed was a mess of unmade decisions when Amory appeared at the foot of the ladder to the loft above me. I started. Was he *choosing* to brave my electric fence? Unable to sense it? Brows raised in wary hope, he stuttered out that he'd come to say goodbye.

I nodded, saying nothing.

He stepped past the ladder. "Can I give you a hug? This one last time?"

A defensive pulse erupted in my chest, frying any urge I might have felt toward tenderness. I couldn't soften now. Come morning, I'd enter a war zone.

"No," I said. His face crumpled. He turned and left the shed.

What if I'd said yes? Would I have dissolved in tears? Let him comfort me? Let his warm hands stroke my wild head? Would he have offered to leave with me? Would I have agreed?

I'd steal my final glimpse of him the next morning. He'd be amid the group in the living room, winning an approving nod and smile from Arol for revealing that he, like Wulf, had encountered Science of Mind as a child. I would think, *It's a good thing I'm going. I must have been keeping him from coming into his own.*

I would be wrong. Within a month or so of my departure for Idaho, he, too, would be gone.

By the time I'd subdued the sleeping bag and zipped up my backpack, mine was the only lamp still lit. My roommates were asleep or on dates. Even the creature who nightly scratched and scuffled within our walls had fallen silent.

I sat on the edge of my bed and surrendered to dread. I was set to leave the Farm in a matter of hours. I had no money and no time to ask my mother for any. My brother lived more than two thousand miles away.

What the fuck am I doing? How the hell am I gonna get myself across the country and back? Am I nuts?

I unzipped my pack and pulled out my *Zendik Book of Scriptures*, then switched off my lamp, crept out the door, and made for the Farmhouse living room, where I could be sure of solitude this far past midnight. I had to escape my sleeping roommates, the static of their tacit condemnation.

On the couch flanking the picture window—blackness

behind me, a smudge of lamp glow in my lap—I read the *Book of Scriptures*, front to back.

I wasn't seeking advice in Wulf's words. I'd long since accepted the text's opacity, telling myself it would reveal its secrets someday, when I achieved the X-ray vision I attributed to Arol and Swan. Rather, I read for the meditation of turning page after page.

Soothed by Wulf's thick yet slippery prose, I opened to new thoughts, which coupled and recoupled without my supervision until they'd birthed what seemed like a plausible solution.

By the time I closed the book, I knew what to do come dawn.

At first light—early enough that I was almost certain to find Arol alone in the Addition kitchen—I slipped out of the Potato Shed and up the terrace steps through the vined pergola crowning her rioting flower beds. In the front hall, I paused to calm my breath, before creeping past the schoolroom to the kitchen. Should I lose my nerve, I didn't want her wondering whose footsteps she'd heard.

The door stood ajar. I knocked.

"Come in!" she called.

She sat facing me, in her robe of royal purple, sections of the *Charlotte Observer* layering the kitchen table. Her hair hung loose around her shoulders. The rising sun brightened the leaves of the linden tree at the window behind her. She raised her teacup to her lips and sipped.

I stopped just inside the doorway. She didn't motion me to sit down or come closer.

"I'm going to Idaho for two weeks. To see the mountains."

"What, do you need a vacation?"

We both knew only squares took vacations. Why would anyone lucky enough to live at the Farm *want* a break from our rustic oasis? Still—maybe her X-ray vision would reveal the love beneath my choice to leave: I'd lost heart for Zendik, through *my* fault. I wouldn't burden it with my misery. Instead, I'd disappear and find a fix, then return cleared to love it better, surrender with joy to its every need.

"Yes," I said, "and I was wondering if I could take three hundred dollars' worth of ammo to sell in Asheville." Three hundred dollars would cover a round-trip bus ticket to Boise, with something left over for food.

She nodded, lips in a flat line. Her gaze cut to the doorway behind me. Fresh footfalls in the hall signaled the end of our audience. I turned to go, hoping my story would hold.

[chapter 8]

Hunting Season

THAT AFTERNOON IN ASHEVILLE, my travel plan unraveled.

Selling alone was like going naked in a dream: Though no one notices you forgot to put your clothes on, you still feel shamefully exposed. How was I to approach strangers with neither the cloak of the first person plural nor the cover story of saving the world?

Normally, I would have said, "We're a bunch of artists, we live on a farm, we think the world's fucked up, so we're starting a revolution. We get donations for our art—it's how we keep our farm going." I would not have used the word "I"; "I" did not matter. Now, I was it. But I didn't make for an inspiring pitch: "I live on this farm about an hour from here, but lately things have been rough, so now I'm raising money for a bus ticket."

Early in the evening, it started to rain. I quit with $67 in my pocket. Sheltering in the doorway of a closed storefront, I faced the obvious, with fear and excitement: I could still make Boise in the next few days. But I would have to hitchhike.

I'd thumbed rides before, both to save money and reach out-of-the-way places. I knew that the currency of hitchhiking

125

was sociability: once drivers got to know and like you, they might go the extra mile or two, feed you, offer you a place to sleep. I also knew that hitching could be risky. Plenty of drivers had picked me up, they'd said, to keep me from predators ready to pounce on a woman alone.

The distance from Asheville to Boise far exceeded any I'd hitched in the past—and my years at the Farm seemed to have prepared me for just such a leap. Selling could have been boot camp for stranger engagement. Plus, the law of psychic cause and effect held that I could repel danger by policing my vibrations. So long as I stayed tied to Zendik—source of love and truth—I'd be safe. I'd attract attack only if my link to Zendik frayed.

Other hitchhikers had told me that if you wanted to book it cross-country, truckers were your best bet. They took speed and drove all night (the legend went), and when your paths diverged they could get on their CB radios and find you an onward ride. Theoretically, flagging down one semi could set you up for a couple thousand miles.

My sources—all male—either had not known or had not told me the whole story.

The first trucker to pick me up, on I-40 near Asheville, offered me a hundred bucks for a blow job. I demanded that he stop the truck and let me out. He backed off and apologized, protesting that some women *did* sell sex out on the highway. Near Nashville, he got me an onward ride.

Another trucker suggested I get some rest while he drove. Exhausted—and expecting him to drive all night, on speed—I stretched out, fully clothed, on the bed in the back of the cab. A couple hours later, at a rest stop in Kansas, he stripped and lay down next to me. I stiffened. What did he want? Would he grab me if I tried to climb out? Within minutes, he was snoring. I squirmed against the cab's back wall, clearing a sliver of buffer between his skin and my clothes, then inched over him into the front seat and tried the door. It opened. My pack was at my feet, where I'd left it. At dawn, I slipped back to the road.

Halfway across Nebraska, I found a ride all the way to Ogden, Utah—just hours south of Boise—with a married Christian who sincerely and unsanctimoniously embraced the chance to praise Jesus by caring for a sister in need. When we shared the bed in his cab overnight, he kept his clothes on and gave me all the space he could. In our eight hundred miles together, he did nothing to breach my trust.

In Logan, Utah—just north of Ogden—I wrapped my arms around the waist of a shy young Harley driver who did ninety the last three hundred miles to Boise. Straddling the wide seat made my butt ache. Desperation to straighten my legs crazed me. Our hurricane-force hurtle turned my cheeks to sandpaper. Yet I liked pressing my chest against the man's back, lacing my fingers over his stomach. Pretending lothario lurked beneath his second skin of black leather.

After a few days with my brother in Boise, I took off by thumb for the mountains, eager to draw the wisdom I craved from the Sawtooths. I might yet return to the Farm within two weeks, my story of Zendik as true love intact.

Shortly past noon on day ten of my trip, I leaned into the last, steep steps to the saddle that would show me Sawtooth Lake. The hip belt on my backpack dug into my stomach; my bulky bedroll bumped against the back of my head. I breathed in deep swallows, as my thighs, butt, and calves clamored for oxygen. Sweat mingled with unscented deodorant in whiffs of whey and rain pipe. I stared down at the grit and pebble of the trail.

At the saddle, I stopped and looked out. The lake's granite banks rose to snowcapped peaks and plunged mine-shaft-deep beneath a sky clouded only by a few poufs of cumulus. This, in light of a text I knew by heart, was holy ground.

On the bus to Idaho in summer 1996 (my first working at Redfish), I'd read *Into the Wild*, Jon Krakauer's just-published account of a young man's quest to survive alone in the Alaskan wilderness. In an epigraph to its epilogue—from Annie Dillard's *Holy the Firm*—I'd found a wisp of mystery that I'd taken as my booklet of revelation and eventually printed, from memory, on the first page of the journal I'd brought to Zendik:

We sleep to time's hurdy-gurdy; we wake, if we ever wake, to the silence of God. And then, when we wake to the deep shores of time uncreated, then when the dazzling dark breaks over the far slopes of time, then it's time to toss things, like our reason, and our will; then it's time to break our necks for home.

There are no events but thoughts and the heart's hard turning, the heart's slow learning where to love and whom. The rest is merely gossip, and tales for other times.

For me, the shores before me—the shores of Sawtooth Lake—were "the deep shores of time uncreated." Surely they would show me where to love and whom. Surely they would free me to break my neck for home.

At the far end of the lake lay a broad, flat boulder, on an emerald carpet stitched with wildflowers. I slipped my thumbs under the shoulder straps of my backpack and set out, boots crunching against scree, for that spot.

On the rock I dropped my pack, leaden with unsold ammo, and sank into a cross-legged hunch. The sun warmed my braid and neck. Granite nubs poked my ankle bones. From the canyon at my back wafted hiker twitter and birdsong. Alone at last, in an expanse immune to human comment, I let my gaze drift out over the lake.

Images coalesced and dissolved on its vast, glassy surface. The Harley's throttle twisting under the driver's grip. The surprise on the one familiar face I'd found the night before in the

Redfish kitchen. The kind eyes of the man who'd treated me to dinner in the Redfish restaurant.

Chad's appearance hadn't changed in the four years since I'd last seen him: he wore the same white chef's coat, the same jaded-yet-sincere smile tinged with sneer. Mine had: I'd traded my baggy black polo shirt and frumpy cotton skirt for a tank that hugged my breasts and pants that hugged my hips. When I told him I'd joined an artists' commune, he nodded in approval. "I don't know much about artists' communes, but that place must be treating you pretty good, 'cause you look great."

Dinner brought another reversal, another subtle triumph. In my two and a half seasons behind the scenes at Redfish— scrubbing pots, slinging salads, flipping eggs—I'd nursed a string of secret crushes while envying my comrades their late-night hook-ups, their summer flings. Now, here I was, on the flip side of the swinging doors, enjoying a Bow-Thai salad across from a handsome man.

Fargo had picked me up in his white Bronco on the out-skirts of Idaho City, a faded mining town. He, too, was bound for Stanley, the village near Redfish that called itself the Gate-way to the Sawtooths. A homesteader seeking a master's in English at Boise State, he moved and spoke with equal grace.

When the conversation in the Bronco turned to Zendik, he enraged me by interrogating each of my sweeping state-ments. How did I *know* that Ecolibrium was the future? That lying caused ecocide? That the world would be healed if every-one lived as we did at the Farm? As I reddened, he remained calm. Finally, I dropped the subject, taking my pain as proof that the entire line of inquiry was a lie.

At dinner, I reveled in the soft glow of the pine walls, varnished to a warm gold, while savoring the gentle thrill of attention from a man who was attractive, articulate, respect-ful (if blind to the beauty of Zendik), and single. This wasn't exactly a date—Fargo had offered to pay for me only after I'd pled poverty—but it was still the closest I'd come to my pre-Zendik fantasy of a guy taking me out to dinner and a movie. And though I couldn't muzzle my inner critic, I knew no one would pounce with input the moment we left the dining room. Back at our campsite on the banks of the Salmon, he repaired to his tent, I to my sleeping bag. The night was clear, the river's rush a gentle roar.

The next morning, with rain forecast later in the day, he urged me to borrow his tent for my trek into the wilderness. He'd sleep in his car by the river; he was just going fishing. I refused. I liked him but wouldn't thread myself, even by so fine a line, to a man who rejected Zendik. I did give him a magazine, when we parted at the Iron Creek Trailhead, on the off chance that it might reach him.

Gazing deeper into my dimming looking glass, I watched storm clouds mass over the mountains and wondered if I'd been wrong to shun Fargo's offer. I saw myself hitching a ride to his hidden driveway, knocking on his cabin door. Him grinning in pleased surprise, inviting me in. Me stepping over the threshold, easing my pack to the floor, warming up under a cloak of welcome and wood smoke.

It was too late. I'd refused the tent. I would not knock on Fargo's door for no reason. What mattered was the quickening I felt spinning this fantasy—and the lethargy that stiffened me when I imagined speeding back to the Farm.

The lake would yield no miracle cure for my break with Zendik. Rather, it seemed to be showing me the contours of an ordeal more arduous than reaching the Sawtooths: playing out—and laying to rest—my Deathculture desire to mate in the wild.

On a blazing afternoon in late July, Eric and I crouched outside an ice cream shop in Davis, California, plucking small crimson fruits from the scorching sidewalk and dropping them into a plastic bag he'd grabbed from the basket of his tandem. Now a PhD candidate in mathematics at UC Davis, Eric had once been my classmate at Harvard. I'd called him from my brother's apartment in Boise, then hitched across the Sierra Nevada to meet him.

In four years at Davis, Eric had learned how to fruit-hunt. We'd already gleaned grapes, figs, and peaches from the grounds of Village Homes, a local cohousing development, and more peaches from a university orchard. Biking back to his place, we'd spotted a constellation of oozing goo-splats, reddish-purple against the gray cement. The fruits were strange to both of us. Cherries didn't splat like that, but, for lack of a better name, we called them cherries.

Our bag was filling rapidly. Eric rocked back on his heels and held it up by its handles. Purple juice pooled in one corner.

"What are we gonna do with all these?" He swung the bag. More juice oozed into the pool. "We could make a pie or something."

"No! It would be a shame to cook them. They're already so amazing." The fruit's dense, licorice-sweet flesh was like nothing I'd ever tasted.

"But we have so many. If we try to eat them all raw, we'll get sick. Or they'll rot."

"Not necessarily. I mean, there's breakfast, lunch, and dinner."

Eric shrugged, dimples punctuating his soft smile. He closed the bag and nestled it beside the other fruits in his basket.

I smiled back. I knew I was being eccentric—and I knew he could handle it. Since its start eight years earlier, our relationship—friendship? what was it?—had been a study in eccentricity.

We'd met at an ice cream social in September 1994, during our first week at Harvard. After running through the getting-to-know-you formula—where are you from, where do you live, what do you plan to concentrate in—we alit on a common interest in philosophy. He explained (though I did not absorb) the meanings of the terms "epistemology" and "ontology." I was impressed by his reserve, his thoughtfulness, his determination to push meaning into each word.

Yet we didn't speak again till the following spring—when he sent me a letter, via university mail, praising an essay I'd written for the *Harvard Salient*. In the essay, "Thinking About Talking," I'd shredded the getting-to-know-you game, claiming, "I'd rather not talk than have a meaningless conversation," and pled for a fresh round of questions: "Who are you?" "What matters to you?" "Why are you here?" In his letter, Eric echoed my sentiments and declared, "Now I am even more certain that you are who I thought you were." I didn't ask who he thought I was—a fellow misanthrope? a deep thinker? his soul mate? I embraced the good news that my writing had reached someone—that I, too, had made an impression.

In response, I knocked on the door of his dorm room shortly before midnight and asked if he wished to go walking. He said yes, and we ended up trekking twenty-six miles, roundtrip, to the suburb of Bedford. We barely spoke—maybe the impossibly high bar we'd set in writing had left us too self-conscious to start a conversation—but for more than six hours I tuned to his movements, hearkened to his breath, matched the quick rhythm of his steps. By the time we parted, at 6:00 a.m., we'd shared silence and a sunrise and spun an unlikely story.

After that we took more walks, and ate together on occasion. Always, we sank into long spells of silence fraught with risks we didn't take—like touching, like asking who we were to each other. We remained ellipses, locked in prolonged elision.

My first night in Davis, we walked out to a cowpen attached to the university agricultural station. At Eric's urging, I climbed with him over the fence. "Stand still and let them come to you. I promise you won't get hurt." One cow approached, then another. Each sniffed me with its wide nostrils, bathed me in its moist breath.

Past the cowpen, at the edge of a wood, we found a downed trunk the length of a love seat and settled on it, a cool breeze whispering through the trees. Our thighs touched. We turned to face each other. With the dark for a cloak, we risked our first kiss. A kiss I owed to Zendik.

If not for my adopted tribe, I would not have sought Eric out. I would not have known how to draw our bodies close. But my learning harbored certain poisons—among them the beliefs that I must drop any man who slowed my evolution, and that love was doomed beyond the Farm.

My first kiss with Eric, I would learn later, was his first kiss ever. I did not promise he would not get hurt.

Mounting the tandem behind him, the afternoon of our cherry harvest, I admired the swell of his shoulders, the sun-bleached hairs arrowing up his sun-browned neck. Had the warmth of California coaxed him into his own? It seemed that he, like the fruit splitting open in his basket, had ripened under the Central Valley's searing rays.

Being with Eric while clinging to Zendik meant stretching the story I'd spun when leaving the Farm: Maybe I'd convert Eric and bring him back with me. Maybe our affair would break me, once and for all, of desiring Deathculture men.

In the meantime, my link to Zendik needed tending. I couldn't risk letting it fray.

Shortly after my arrival in Davis, I called the Farm from a pay phone. I wanted to be ready to return, but I wasn't. And I'd used up my two weeks.

The phone rang once, then twice. My sweat beaded on the receiver. Then—"Hello?" It was Lysis. A relief.

Of all the Zendiks, Lysis was best at empathizing with outsiders. So it often fell to him to negotiate between the Farm's core and its fringe. He listened as I spilled out a summary of my trip so far, then responded with the verbal equivalent of a shrug. "Let us know if you get married or something."

But I couldn't rest my case; I craved judgment. Was I on the right track? If not, how could I find my way back?

"I'll talk to Arol about it," he said. "Call at ten tomorrow morning."

The next morning, early, I took Eric's phone out to his patio and set it on his picnic table, inches from my chest. Following me outside, he sank onto the couch against the back wall of the house. He pulled on a string dangling from a seat cushion. I watched the clock on the phone creep toward 7:00 a.m.

I'd told Eric about the tension I felt between my tie to him and my tie to the Farm. I'd explained why it was futile to seek true love in a culture built on lies, without the guidance of an insulating tribe. If he challenged me, he did so gently. Maybe he feared scaring me off. Maybe he saw the allure of my story, despite its gaps. Or maybe he, like me, excelled at supplying coherence to a ragbag of notions promoted as facts.

At the edge of the yard, sunlight dappled a garden bed through the leaves of an apple tree. Honeybees buzzed from clumps of cherry-tomato flowers to sprays of apple blossoms, sipping from both. Was there any way I might combine interest in Eric with commitment to Zendik? Draw nectar from more than one source? Might Arol zap my tension in a flash of wisdom?

As 6:59 flipped to 7:00, I dialed the number I knew by heart. Again, Lysis answered, with an upbeat "hello!"

Through the receiver filtered laughter and chatter, footfalls on stairs. Probably he was in the Addition office, just two doors down from Arol's kitchen. Was she within earshot? Would others in the room pause to listen to his end of our conversation? Did they care what I was up to? Did anyone miss me?

"Hi, Lysis. This is Helen."

His tone flattened. "Yeah. Helen. Um . . ."

I dug my thumbnail into the picnic table. I wondered if

my banana boxes full of stuff were still under my bed in the Potato Shed. I waited, half-hoping he'd finish his sentence, half-hoping he'd suspend it. I heard only the puff of his breath.

"Um, sorry, but I can't really talk except to let you know that Arol said don't call and don't come back until you wanna be a Zendik."

I remained silent. Tears rose in my eyes. My only defense.

Lysis cleared his throat. "Okay, well, gotta go, Helen. Maybe we'll see you again sometime. Bye."

I dropped the receiver into its cradle. The numbers on the clock blurred. I turned to Eric. He was leaning toward me, alert for a verdict. "Arol said don't call and don't come back—"

My voice broke. I pushed the phone away. I nested my face in my forearms, as sobs racked my body.

I still believed I'd gone out to renew my commitment to Zendik. I could no longer pretend Zendik agreed.

I didn't take comfort in Eric's move to the table to put his arm around me.

I didn't revive when we hunted fruit that afternoon or drove to the redwoods a couple days later.

Parked in a lot by a radiant glade, we stared through the windshield at a world thick with fog.

He glanced at me, then back at the windshield. "So, why'd you come here, anyway?"

I turned to look at him. He squinted into the mist. I turned away.

"Because it felt right. And because I always thought of you as someone who was just as frustrated as I was with all the superficial bullshit."

Fog drifted over us, obscuring both rear view and mirror.

"But is there any chance you could stay and we could have a relationship?"

"There *is* a chance we could have a relationship—but only if we both lived at Zendik."

Blood rushed to his cheeks. He swiveled toward me. I forced myself to face him. My gaze scraped against his.

"Are you serious? Is that what you *really* think?"

I nodded.

"So, you came all the way out here to see me and get my hopes up, and the whole time you were sure it was never gonna work." His lips tightened. His hand made a fist. "It's like . . . it's like this was some kind of *experiment*. Right? Except you already knew how it was gonna turn out."

I stared into my lap, at my own curled fingers. I looked back up at him. "Yeah, I guess," I said, tears blurring my vision. "I'm sorry, Eric. I try to follow my heart, but right now I can't feel it. I thought we could try to be honest with each other on our own, and then maybe you'd wanna go back to the Farm with me."

"I'm not going back to your damn farm!" He punched the padded ridge dividing his seat from mine. "But I don't understand why we can't try to be together, just the two of us, right here!"

I dropped my eyes back to my hands—clenched into claws, hunting a grip.

"I can't, Eric. I just can't. I feel like if I did, I'd . . . I'd shrivel up."

Back at my brother's place in Boise, I learned I'd been admitted to the September visitor group at East Wind—the Missouri commune over which I'd chosen Zendik in October 1999. I was to arrive at East Wind no earlier than the end of August.

To kill a few weeks—and a couple more dreams—I hitched to Alaska by way of Glacier National Park.

In Glacier, from the backseat of a sleek rental car, I watched a husband on honeymoon release the wheel to clasp his wife's gold-banded hand. Twisting his innocent gesture into a death grip, I imagined him hissing, *You're mine, all mine*—and took this as a good sign: maybe I'd finally iced my desire to mate in the wild.

In British Columbia, a trucker hauling timber to Alberta pushed me repeatedly to take a nap in the back of his cab. After refusing half a dozen times, I lied that I had to pee and asked him to stop at a gas station. Instead, he dropped me off, after midnight, on a desolate street at the edge of Prince George. I made it till morning with the help of a cashier at a twenty-four-hour 7-Eleven who unlocked her minivan so I could sleep a few hours in the backseat.

In Anchorage, I found purple-leaved trees like the one that had showered Eric and me with "cherries"—really ornamental plums—in Davis. But they yielded only tiny, tasteless pellets. The plums I picked in Osoyoos, Washington, were larger but still hard and tart. None of the fruit I hunted on my own proved half as luscious as the plums we'd bagged together.

When I returned to Boise, in late August, I was exhausted—and leery of hitching to East Wind. My thread to Zendik—which I believed had delivered me from harm so far—thinned as my absence lengthened. I assumed that by now my banana boxes had been shunted to the barn or shoved deep under the bed to make way for another Zendik's claim on my space. That those who wove the Zendik story had recast me as a traitor, or a ghost.

I gladly accepted my brother's offer of a bus ticket. From Springfield, Missouri, I'd hitch the final ninety miles to Tecumseh, where someone from East Wind would meet me.

The trouble was that the bus wouldn't reach Springfield till 5:00 p.m.—leaving me just a couple hours' daylight to complete my trip.

I'd be fine, I told myself. It was only ninety miles.

From the Springfield bus stop, I should have hiked south to the edge of town, where I might have found a good spot—a broad shoulder, a turnout—and drivers headed for Tecumseh.

But I feared losing time, and I was tired. So I trudged up a hill to a busy commercial strip and settled for sticking my thumb out in the wide driveway of a Pizza Hut.

At about six o'clock, in a battered blue Honda, Alvin Long pulled up.

He said sure, he'd take me to Tecumseh—he just had an errand to run before we hit the road. He gave me a crumpled dollar bill and some change and told me to go inside and get a soda.

I didn't drink soda. And I'd formed the habit of hoarding every penny I received for health-food-store purchases or emergencies. I pocketed the money and sipped from my water bottle.

I sensed something amiss in Alvin's instructions—why hadn't he left me in the driveway and promised to pick me up if I was still there when he returned?—but I was too beat to put my finger on it.

I didn't start to worry till he ignored a sign for US-65 and turned instead onto a lettered byway. A stack of cards in a niche between us identified him as a stump remover serving the Springfield area. Surely he must know the local roads.

"Is *this* the way to Tecumseh? I thought we were supposed to take Highway Sixty-Five."

He stared straight ahead and tightened his grip on the wheel. His scalp reddened under his buzz cut.

"Look, I told you I'd take you there. You wanna get out and walk?"

Indeed I did not. The lettered road had led into a lettered labyrinth. If I left now, I'd be lost, with no ride at all. So I made up a story: *He's taking a shortcut.*

But he wasn't in a hurry. He stopped twice to chat with homeowners mowing stump-infested lawns. After his second sales pitch, he returned to the car and stood by my window. I rolled it all the way down. "Hey, you know how to drive?" he asked.

"I've driven before, but I don't really know how and I don't have a license."

A friend of my brother's had taken me driving in the hills above Boise. Fargo had let me drive his Bronco partway to Stanley. Both men had been kind and patient, bearing with my vise grip on the wheel, my terror of accelerating beyond twenty miles an hour.

"What are you waiting for? Let's switch. I'll give you a lesson."

"Um, I don't really want to." I'd already seen Alvin lose his cool. And I preferred not to fool around, now that the sun was sinking.

"Come on! It'll be fun. Just do it!"

He opened my door and shooed me out. I drove a few miles through the maze while he teased me for going slow and stopping short at intersections. The further delay worried me, but I liked being teased. It reminded me of Zendik, where my peers knew me well enough to poke fun at my quirks.

After Alvin took the wheel back, we passed a jeep parked in a clearing by a creek, packed with young men drinking beer. He slowed to wave at them and shouted something I couldn't make out. They raised their beer cans and leered back at him. I clung to my story: *Any second now, I'll see a sign for the highway.*

Around 7:00 p.m., Alvin stopped on a wooded road, out of sight of any houses.

"Gotta pee," he said. He got out and strolled toward the rear of the car.

Out my window, the sun streaked the sky orange as it crept behind a ragged horizon. Right by the road, a kudzu vine lassoed a slender trunk—reminding me, again, of Zendik. In the warmer climate of North Carolina, kudzu was known to choke whole forests. Though still hundreds of miles from the Farm, I was closer than I'd been since mid-July.

Gravel crunched under Alvin's feet. He took his seat and slammed the door. *Finally. Now we can go. I bet we're just a turn from the Tecumseh road.*

But he didn't start the engine. He arched his back and rolled his shoulders. He raked his fingers through his close-mown hair. *Okay, he's settling in for the rest of the drive.*

He turned to me, lip curled.

He fixed me with a lizard gaze.

"I'll give you a hundred bucks for a blow job," he said.

Blood flooded my face. One hand made a fist. The other gripped it. *I-40 out of Asheville. First trucker.* Same threat. Same offer.

"No. *No way.*"

He grabbed me. Shoved his tongue through my teeth. Seized my breast. A scream thrust up. He caught it. "I got a knife. You scream and I'll cut you. Don't make me cut you."

I whimpered. Shivered. Shook. Squirmed to free an inch between us. He squeezed me tighter. *What? No! Got out last time. Way out now. Way out now.*

Fingers. Clutching my back. Stubby insults. Hand on my breast. Hand like cardboard, rough and dead. Tongue in my mouth. Lizard tongue. *Why? WHY?*

I jerked my head back, freed my tongue. "Why? Why are you doing this?"

He froze for an instant, let go an inch. I dove for my door, grabbed the handle. Pulled. *No.* Locked. Power locks. Switch on his side.

Window. Open. All the way open. Head through, neck through, chest through, hips through, butt through, legs through.

Out. All the way out.

The engine growled. He hauled my pack up from the backseat and pushed it through the window. Drove off in a haze of red dust. I lifted my pack and slipped my arms through the straps. Fastened the hip belt. Walked.

Around the next bend stood a ranch house flanked by a wide, fenced lawn. *Maybe they'll let me roll out my sleeping bag on the grass for the night.* I climbed the porch steps and rang the bell, planning to ask. A woman pulled the door open. Jaw taut, cheeks rouged, hair puffed. Eyes hard with mistrust.

"Yes?"

My plan collapsed. I sobbed out a sketch of the attack.

She waved me into her gleaming kitchen and retrieved her cordless phone. "Do you want me to call the police?" she asked, finger poised above the keypad.

"Yes. Please."

One of the policemen chatted with the woman while the other transcribed my story, starting at six o'clock at the Pizza Hut in Springfield, ending an hour later in the midst of a maze. It seemed vital to me that the man in the navy uniform with the gun at his hip should record, on lined paper, every detail I could remember. By the time he finished, my eyes were dry.

I no longer wished to rest on the wide green lawn. The woman's jaw was still taut, her eyes still hard. By now it was dark. The officer who'd recorded my story offered me a ride— but not as far as Tecumseh.

"County police, ma'am. Best we can do is get you to the county line."

They dropped me at a gas station, where I met two young men who said I could spend the night in their spare room, a short walk from the Tecumseh road. They were kind, high, solicitous. Incensed by Alvin's trespass.

Alone in the dark, plagued by waking nightmares of scaly predators stealing in from the hall or out from under the bed, I studied the assault through the warped lens of psychic cause and effect.

Why had I wanted it?

Had I regressed to hunting forced touch after half a summer starved of sex, among friends?

Or was I hot to shock myself back to Zendik? In the weeks since Arol's ultimatum, I had not wanted to call the Farm and beg another chance. But oh, how I'd *wanted* to want to. How I wanted that now.

I'd heard Arol say that people didn't change when they went out; at best, they grew more desperate to flee the Death-culture. Perhaps my corruption ran so deep that I would never return out of zeal for Zendik's crusade to save the world, or hope for Friendship unto Love. Perhaps I'd *required* a threat to my survival.

The assault, I decided, bore a warning: head back or risk death.

I arrived at East Wind primed for signs of decay.

In the morning, making guacamole for the commune's lunch, I discovered that most of the avocados in the walk-in were rotten. Then, hiding out in the visitors' kitchen, I found ants parading bits of amaranth flake over the lip of a box left open. Finally, on a tour of the nut-butter factory, my guide—a shirtless hippie with the taut paunch and scarlet flush of a hard drinker—highlighted the residue griming the production line. He said I could help deep-clean the factory's machinery over the weekend, if I wanted to.

I didn't want to. I couldn't *grasp* wanting to. How could such a task be attractive to *anyone*? (Was that where the hard drinking came in?) I saw the machinery—unless it attracted an ant army—going uncleaned.

I had other scrubbing to do. The assault lay like a smudge on my breast, a sooty clutch print. I needed a woman to talk to. I needed help to wash it off.

Back at the visitors' house, I repaired to the living room and sank into the worn armchair by the phone. I did not call the Farm. I called my mother, collect, and poured out my story, sobbing afresh. As she listened with warm concern, the mark started to fade. Some of my vigor returned.

Maybe I was strong enough to make that other call.

Maybe I was ready to break my neck for Zendik.

Early the next morning, I climbed down from my sleeping loft and marched, heart pounding, to the phone. It was Saturday, August 31. Soon, more seekers would arrive. For now, the house was still.

I lifted the receiver and pressed the eleven digits that would link me to Zendik.

The phone rang. Once. Twice. Three times. Then, the *thwip* of a receiver lifting. A voice—throaty, unmistakable—I was not prepared to hear.

"Hello?"

"Hi, this is Helen. Is Lysis there?"

A dry snort. "Lysis? What? This is Arol. You wanna come back, you gotta go through *me*."

"I *do* want to come back," I said, voice cracking. "I want to be a Zendik." I knew not to mention the assault or recap my absence. Arol didn't care what had prompted my call.

She breathed, waited a beat. "I don't think you'd fit in here. Since you left, we've been getting closer. Building kick-ass relationships. All of us. *You* wanna run your own show."

"Please," I pled, through tears. *"Please. I just want one more chance."*

My sobs turned to ragged gasps. I slumped forward and stared at my feet. An ant approached my bare toes.

Arol took another breath.

"Okay. One more chance," she said.

My mother agreed to wire money for a bus ticket. Sure, she might have preferred to pay my fare to New York—but she'd settle for sparing herself more stories like the one she'd heard the day before.

On the bus that afternoon, forehead pressed to a fogged pane, I imagined the end I might have met, had I succumbed to the Deathculture. In my vision, I crawled back to Alvin, for round after round of ever more brutal abuse. I died a battered hag, keening through chipped teeth as a broomstick cracked against my crown.

With this strand of fantasy, I sought to squeeze the last gasp from my desire to mate in the wild.

On another bus, a couple years earlier—returning to Zendik from my visit to Brooklyn—I'd dreamed that I'd dumped Kro for a lean, flint-jawed man, singed with rage and danger, and that Kro had chided me with a wistful plea: "Didn't you know I offered you a friendship, Helen?" I wondered now: Could I have sidestepped Alvin, could I have bypassed this stretch as an outcast, if I'd stuck with the first Zendik who'd wooed me? Had I been wrong to seek spark and warmth in a single flame?

By morning I was just twenty miles east of the Farm, waiting for a Zendik to retrieve me from Spindale. As a half hour stretched to one hour, then two, I wondered if I would need to surrender what little cash I had to Discount Taxi—and recalled my four-hour wait for a ride from the Hendersonville bus stop, in October 1999. That time, I'd believed the delay had nothing to do with me.

This time, I knew better.

[chapter 9]

Invading the Body

THE STORY THAT I WOULD DIE if I couldn't be a Zendik had thrust me back to the Farm.

Could it power me through the immune response roused by my return?

I idled at the end of a long butcher block in the Farm's new kitchen, craving recognition. This kitchen, nearly complete when I'd left, had shifted into service while I'd been gone. It stood uphill from the Farmhouse and across from the Addition. Morning sun poured through enormous windows, stretching toward a soaring ceiling. I had not crawled under a counter. Yet the dozen Zendiks at work nearby—dusting glassware, clearing breakfast, straining cheese—seemed not to see me.

Maybe they awaited word of what to see.

A door banged. I turned toward it. Arol advanced through the pantry, Prophet at her back. She stopped at the doorsill and pushed her palms against the jambs. Her silver hair spilled past the rim of her shimmering robe.

I folded my arms over my chest and ground my heel against a ridge in the flagstone floor. Her lips twisted into a grimace. "*That* was quick."

I nodded. I *had* traveled fast. This I took as psychic proof that I'd been right to come back. But Arol seemed to be casting me as an intruder who'd dashed through a gate left unlatched by mistake.

"You look good," she continued, stepping toward me and passing a hand, aslant, across her face. "Kind of clear and open. Like you've been going through it."

I nodded again, letting myself hope, for a moment, that we agreed: I'd gone out so I could love Zendik better. Clear myself for full surrender.

"Won't last, though." She chuckled. "Knowing you, you'll be fucked up and shut down in no time."

Prophet stepped forward and squeezed her shoulder. I forced a weak smile—as if mimicking her amusement might mark me as self. Assure her we belonged to one body.

She was not assured.

The next day, after lunch, the body attacked.

Prophet and Zar commanded armchairs flanking the door from the living room out to the porch. The rest of the group—save Arol and the kids—filled the couches, the other chairs, the floor. I huddled on the rug a few feet from Prophet. No one had told me the goal of the meeting. No one would meet my eyes.

I folded my legs and pressed my elbows against my knees. I studied the rug. I looked up.

Prophet tugged at his goatee. Outside, a peahen squawked. A peacock answered. He stilled the crowd with a nod.

"A lot of us up the hill are feeling like it was a bad idea to have Helen come back. We gave it a shot, and it didn't work out. No hard feelings, but we think she should go. She's not cut out to be a Zendik."

Shure chimed in from the couch behind me. "I get this competitive vibe from her about the new kitchen. She was supposed to help set it up, then she left. Now she won't give anyone else credit. I haven't heard her say one nice thing about it."

"Yeah," said Karma. "I'm not even sure why she made the trip. I didn't feel good about seeing her again. Nobody did. That's why I couldn't find her a ride from Spindale. Psychically we all knew what she'd be like. I'm all for second chances and people changing—but Helen is a *long* shot."

Prophet slapped a mosquito against his arm. Zar cleared his throat and turned to Lysis. "Remember the old days, Lys? When Wulf used to tell people, 'You have five minutes to decide'? You got thrown up against it, you had to spit it out. I say Helen gets five minutes."

Lysis nodded. So did Prophet. Then he looked my way, for the first time that afternoon. "Helen, where are you at?"

Fear of exile surged from gut to throat to mouth, crashed against the remembered trespass of Alvin's lizard tongue. If I left again, whose prey would I become?

"I want to be here," I quavered. Tears mustered in my ducts. Surely they would back me up.

"I don't believe her," said Karma, cheeks scrunched in scorn. "She cries all the time. It means nothing."

Prophet shifted in his chair. Squeezed the armrest. "How about this. She has half an hour to go off by herself and decide. One half hour. That's it."

With that he shed the role of surrogate executioner—and reprieved me, briefly, from scrutiny.

He rose to leave. The crowd rose with him. No one checked a clock or set a timer. Who would track my half hour?

I bolted out the back door and down the path through the woods to the outhouse. I fastened the latch, then closed the toilet lid and sank onto it, mouth-breathing to shut out the sour scent of shit rising from the ten-foot chute.

What should I do? If I were doubt-free, this ultimatum would not have come for me. Yet leaving again, in my story, meant dropping to an end as dead and foul as the floor of the shithole.

I couldn't force out doubt in half an hour. But I could feign certainty as I beat a path back to the Farm's heart.

After what seemed like thirty minutes, I made for the dance room, where Swan was leading a class packed with my peers. Neither Arol nor Zar nor Prophet would be there. If I could convince Swan, I was in.

I crept up the steps and peeked through the fanlight in the door. Swan was leading a few rows of dancers in a sequence of kicks. She glistened with sweat; they pulsed red with the fight to keep up.

I had to sync with that beat.

I turned the knob and slipped inside, heart pounding twice as fast as Swan's count. She paused. The door clicked shut behind me.

"I decided I want to stay."

Her eyes narrowed. "Are you sure?"

"Yes. I'm sure."

She waved me forward and resumed her count. Rave and Karma stepped apart to let me in. I seized the beat and kicked.

Zar kicked off the first sex meeting of the fall with a recap of the pattern set during my absence: at each of the past few meetings, one or two people had either volunteered or been chosen to have their sexuality critiqued. "Who wants input this time?" he asked.

I seized the chance.

In the month since my return, I'd failed to weave myself back into the dating scene. Most of the men seemed wary of my otherness—fearful it was contagious. Kro had said no when I'd hit him up for a walk the previous week. I expected the input to sting; I hoped it would help web me in.

I'd gone on at least a walk with most of the men in the circle on the floor of the Mobile (now the music room, where Zar reigned as recording engineer). But I'd managed multiple dates with only a few and tried a relationship only with Kro. Amory had left the Farm soon after I had. Owen, another ex-boyfriend, had left in spring 2001. Of all the men present, Kro knew me best.

He reported, to nods from other men, that I liked kissing and making out but was cock-shy, and stiff during sex—a frustrating lay, in short. Of course his judgment stung. But what crushed me was his flat tone, his blank gaze—he could have been reviewing a toothbrush.

Had I been wrong to take Alvin's lunge as a push toward Kro? Or had I just moved too soon? Maybe, before he would touch me, he'd need proof I belonged.

Arol's sixty-fourth birthday—October 14, 2002—brought news of a siege I could use.

At her party, after dinner in the living room, I was tired but excited. I'd chosen to stay up till dawn finishing my gift: a purple, gold, and cerulean circle-Z embroidered on a square of midnight velvet—and it seemed I'd made the right call. As she opened her presents, she gibed those who'd pledged items to be delivered later: "I want the thing in my hands *now*, goddammit!" She was only half-joking.

When she raised my work to the light and exclaimed, "How pretty!" I flushed with pleasure, glad I'd grabbed this chance to stitch myself into her favor—even as I puzzled over a new chord in her manner: tinny gaiety, shrill with joyless laughter.

After cake, she stilled the room. "I have something to tell you guys," she said. "I went to the doctor this afternoon. They did some tests; I got the results . . ." She paused. We pulsed. A harsh sparkle lit her eyes.

"I have cancer," she said. "It started in my ovaries and spread to this whole area." She circled her abdomen with a half-curled hand. "I'll have to have a hysterectomy."

Once, selling to a graying, middle-aged man under a Savannah overpass, I'd been asked if the law of cause and effect applied to people with cancer. Did they lure it into their bodies, to speed release from lives they couldn't bear? "Yes," I said, ignoring his tight lips, his fierce stare.

The man's jaw clenched. His eyes burned with hurt and hate. "My wife has cancer," he said.

As the shock wave of Arol's revelation broke over me, I flashed on this exchange, then blacked it out. How dare I link her sickness to a Deathculture incident or invoke a pattern used to probe the average pain? Surely her circumstances were singular, and beyond my ken.

A year later, Arol would announce the psychic source of her cancer: overdevotion to the revolution. Her fervor for Earth saving had spurred her to work too hard.

The room whirred with incredulous murmurs. Could it be true that Arol was mortal? She'd seemed superhuman—hot to forge ahead no matter what, suffering others but not needing us.

Two weeks later, at an evening meeting in the Addition kitchen, Arol edged closer than she ever had, in my presence, to declaring her dependence.

She sat with her back against the table, as if to brace herself for the press of the rest of us. Some stood, hugging walls and counters. I squeezed onto the floor a few feet in front of her.

"I'm going to Mexico for a month," she said. "For treatment after my operation." Defiance rumbled underneath her words.

With Karma's help, Arol had found a healing center, just south of the California border, that took a holistic approach to expelling cancer. The center's founder and chief physician, Arol said, had been run out of the US by drug companies guarding their profits.

Challenge flared in her gaze. "It's going to cost twenty-five thousand dollars," she said.

The room throbbed with breath and heartbeat. No one spoke.

Medicare must have been slated to pay for Arol's hysterectomy at a Charlotte hospital; the cost of the surgery never came up. But Medicare didn't cover visits to renegade doctors in Mexico. And $25,000 was a big chunk—roughly what we'd make in five to eight selling weekends. To save herself, Arol needed our help.

Since my return, I'd taken charge of tending the "sickies"—those shunted to the trailer, supposedly to keep bugs at bay. (They spread anyway.) Time in the trailer meant eons alone, with little to do but wonder how you'd caused yourself to fall ill—and agonize over what theories might be roaming the Farm. You could go a day or more without visitors, especially if you were single or your relationship was suspected of making you sick. Defenses down, you embraced any care offered—meals, news, herbal remedies—even by a fellow outcast.

Arol's need for cancer treatment, like the sickies' isolation, warmed her to bonding with the least of her followers—and granted me a chance to help save her life, as I believed she'd saved mine.

I broke the silence. "I don't care how much it costs. I'd sell New Orleans for two weeks straight if it would help you get well."

The room burst into a supportive chorus. "Thank you, Helen," she said.

Days later, New Orleans erupted the muck beneath my pledge.

It was Halloween weekend. I was driving with five other sellers through a city park to Voodoo Fest when I caught myself committing what I saw as thought crime.

Outside, lush meadows rolled by under wet sky. My mind wandered to Arol's battle with cancer. She would have a hysterectomy. She would retreat to Mexico. When she returned, she would start chemo. But none of these tactics guaranteed victory. *What if she dies?*

Thinking that Arol might die was crime enough. Yet I pressed on. How might life at the Farm change in the wake of her death? To my shock, I did not see a flock of lost sheep, stumbling in grief. Instead, I imagined bounding up the steps to the Addition, striding down the hall to the kitchen, without the usual rush of adrenaline. Worse, I imagined asking Prophet for a date—with a chance he'd say yes.

I did not lust after Prophet. I did feel the pull of the one man who shared Arol's grasp of lasting love. What mysteries had enfolded only him?

Mar—the power seller who'd passed out TurboCharge the last day of my first Mardi Gras—pulled into a parking spot near the festival's vendor entrance. I snapped back to the present. When the four men on our crew left to sneak our food and ammo into the venue, I turned to Mar, heart thumping. I had to confess.

"Hey, can I tell you something? I know it's super dumb, but I feel like if I don't let it out, I'll bomb."

Mar was the trip's leader. All she wanted was to call home each morning with a high number.

"Sure," she said. "Go ahead."

I leaped straight to my worst offense. "Well, I just noticed myself having this awful thought—that maybe if Arol died, I'd get to have sex with Prophet. I mean, it's horrible! I don't want Arol to die! But I had that thought, and now it's like this evil growth filling my brain."

Mar twirled a red ringlet around her forefinger. Tugged at the clutch of bogus passes hanging from the mirror. I squirmed, awaiting her verdict.

"Isn't this one of those things you do to sabotage yourself? Aren't you just freaking out about selling?"

I nodded, weak with relief. She'd neither damned me as a traitor nor demanded I leave.

"Don't worry about it. We all have bad thoughts. We

come from a Deathculture." She flashed me a half smile. "We do the best we can."

I smiled back, silently vowing not to trespass again.

Yet I *did* feel more at home, with Arol and most of her inner circle gone. They departed the day after Thanksgiving in a large RV, leaving the rest of us to wonder how we'd bear up without them. Would we go "square"? Cave to our neuroses? Implode? Within days, we knew we'd make it. Within a week, I found that I could indeed visit the Addition with a steady heart. I'd never felt such ease at the Farm.

Midway through December, the home crew started on a collaborative art project: a mockumentary spoofing our fear of losing it. We'd send the finished video to Mexico as a Christmas gift.

In one scene, a new guy who had a crush on Karma knelt in front of a four-by-eight-foot blackboard, mapping her every move with a fresh chalk track. In another, Rayel—our interim financial manager—gaily threw money away. Garbed in a filmy scarf and sparkly earrings, hair swept up in a twist, she sat at Arol's desk with a feathered pen and a checkbook. As strings raced and cymbals crashed, she signed check after check, ripped it from the book, and tossed it with laughter over her shoulder.

I took my star turn in the Tupperware cupboard.

As a young Zendik, I'd appointed myself guardian of the Farm's Tupperware: haphazard stacks of tubs in a range of makes and shapes, a mess of lids shoved in a basket. I hated the last-minute—often late-night—hunt for lids to tubs already filled with road food; I flinched when I saw the wrong lid taped to a tub in the cooler. If only each tub were stored *with its lid on it*, the needless hunt for mates would end.

No! I was told. Space was scarce. Tubs must nest; lids must mix. My best hope was the periodic purge: I'd pull out all the tubs and lids and match what I could, then pack the unpaired off to Tupperware Purgatory (a cardboard box stowed in the Farmhouse) to await their mates' return (largely in vain).

In my scene, I plunged into the jumbled cupboard, swearing I'd have it tidy in no time. A beat later, seeing some lids had gone missing, I fell back in a dead faint.

Before mailing the video to Mexico, we popped it into the Farmhouse VCR and watched it over and over, crying with laughter. It captured our love for each other—and a dream of what life as one body *could* be: we'd joined, with joy, in work we owned.

Arol and company, homesick for the Farm, loved our gift. Swan's boyfriend, Noi, reciprocated with a snappy animation of a line of pink flamingos bopping in lockstep to a rock beat.

The day Arol's RV rolled up the driveway, Prophet touched my arm in the Addition kitchen and thanked me for the rap song I'd penned and taped for his mid-December birthday. I treasured the gentle twinkle in his eyes, humbly meeting mine; I imagined it signaled a merging of inner and outer circles. Might the new year—just begun—bring a new start?

A day or so later, Arol, exhausted and fragile, called me to the pantry doorway. Four months earlier, cutting me with her double-edged greeting, she'd commanded its breadth; now, voice ragged, she sagged against one jamb. "I'd like you to try singing with me," she said, "once I'm well enough to do music again."

"Thank you! I'd love to."

I'd once loved singing in church, and with my mother and sisters at home. I'd long wanted to sing with Arol in the band. But what thrilled me more than her proposal (which would come to little) was the warmth coursing under it—the warmth, at last, of welcome.

[chapter 10]

Untamed Flame

SAUTÉING DINNER VEGGIES IN a cast-iron skillet, I stole glances at Dylan, the visitor Eile had just shown into the kitchen. He looked feral and young. A patchwork coat quilted his bony frame. A coarse headband curbed a riot of curls.

By February 2003, more than three years had passed since my own first supper. Quarantine endured: visitors still had to wait ten days before they could cook, wash dishes, or share the common dishware. Dylan's bowl was labeled, as mine had been, with his name on a strip of masking tape.

The protein that night was baked chicken. At the butcher block, Dylan plucked the lid from a pan of fragrant legs and breasts. Dismay shaded his face. He glanced at Eile, serving herself opposite him. "Um, is there anything besides chicken? I'm a vegetarian."

I turned from the stove and caught his eye for the first time. "I can make you lentil patties," I said.

He smiled. "Thanks. That would be great."

In the dining hall, I chose a seat across from his. Picking the flesh from my chicken leg, I listened to Eile quiz Dylan on how he'd found Zendik.

"I used to post to your online bulletin board. Poems and stuff."
I looked up. "You're Elfdancer. From the Forum."

Arol had started the Zendik Forum—with boards for
Art, Philosophy, and General Questions—in late 2001, expecting a surge of earnest requests for advice from those hoping to
Zendicize their Deathculture lives. Such petitions did trickle
in—along with a stream of criticism, which Arol denounced
as nasty gossip. After about a year, she shut the Forum down.

Elfdancer had posted most often to the Art Forum,
which I'd helped mind. I remembered his wistful paeans to
wild mountain quiet, his impressionistic vision of a diffuse uto-
pia blooming in coffee shops across the nation, his allusions to
through-hiking the Appalachian Trail.

"Yeah," he said, "I'm Elfdancer. From the Forum." His
chin rose in challenge. "Why'd you guys ax it?"

"We got sick of the attacks. Sure, we're not perfect. But
we *are* starting a new culture. Why waste time on a bunch of
losers badmouthing us so they can stay on the couch?"

He shrugged. "*I* thought the back-and-forth was kind of
healthy. But I knew all along that the only way to really get
what was going on here was to see for myself."

I nodded, wondering if I'd psychically drawn him to
visit—if the romantic moonscape I'd been facing had finally
given rise to a tiny green shoot.

At the time of Dylan's arrival, almost every man on the
Farm either had a girlfriend or had recently refused my hit-up.
Even Kro remained cold. Plus, I'd noticed something strange:
though Arol had warned us more than once that sleeping
together exposed couples to ill-defined dangers, more and
more of my Potato Shed roommates were joining their lovers in
other houses for regular sleepovers. Some were even prolonging
dates till morning and slumbering—with the luxury of a double
bed—in the date space.

Arol slept with Prophet, Swan slept with Noi, every night

in double beds in the Treehouse (a cozy log cabin, adjoining the Addition, custom-built for Arol and her intimates). It went without saying that sleeping together was safe for them.

The loft I shared with Eile, under a pitched roof, peaked at about four feet. But it was deep enough to allow each of us a double mattress. The emptier the Potato Shed got, the more I longed for a man to share my bed. If I didn't join the sexual slumber party soon, I thought, I'd miss my chance. I knew it couldn't last.

I had little to lose but my loneliness. Why *not* hit Dylan up for a walk?

A couple nights after his first supper, I caught Karma in the main kitchen and ran my plan by her. Then I marched down the hill to find Dylan. (About a year earlier, Arol had cut out the middle woman, leaving us to proposition each other in person.) En route to the Old Music Room—now the visitors' house—I spotted him on the Farmhouse porch. Heart pounding, I waved and translated my offer into his vernacular: "Hey, I was wondering if you'd wanna hang out with me."

"You mean, do I wanna go on a 'walk'?" he shot back.

"Right."

He smirked, eyes spiked with mischief. "Yeah, I know the lingo."

At the end of the driveway, we turned down Regan Jackson, the faint whoosh of traffic a half mile away on Lake Adger our only cue that we shared the night with other humans. Ever curious about the paths people took to Zendik, I urged him to recount his recent adventures. It turned out he'd through-hiked the Appalachian Trail in 2001 and traveled to Fort Benning, Georgia in late 2002 to join a yearly protest against the US Army's School of the Americas.

I knew of the SOA's reputation for training Latin American troops to crush dissent with violence. I'd once applauded those who risked arrest by "crossing the line" onto SOA property every November. I'd even given the Farm my grant money in part to sidestep a federal Midas whose touch turned gold to war. But my Zendik story fenced out respect for others' answers. So I felt only pity, tinged with irritation, when Dylan told me he'd start a three-month prison term in April.

"I could have gotten out of it," he said, "but I had to stand by what I did. Take the consequences. And I feel like I'll learn something from being in prison. I don't know what, but something."

"Uh-huh," I said. *Dead end.*

"So, do you have a girlfriend?"

We'd passed the neighbor's tidy ranch house. Two horses— one at the fence, one at a distance—nibbled on grass. Dylan ducked his head and mumbled.

"What did you say?"

"I said I'm not sure."

"What do you mean?"

"There's this girl . . . We're taking a break . . . It might be over . . ." He shook his head. "I don't know."

At the edge of the neighbor's pasture stood a pale blue school bus that disappeared farther into the woods each year. It always made me think of Chris McCandless, the man who'd vanished *Into the Wild*. He'd starved to death in an abandoned bus much like this one, unaware of the nearby cable car that could have whisked him over a swollen river to the help of other humans. He would have known the route to reunion—if he'd brought a map.

Just past the school bus, Regan Jackson gave way to an overgrown logging path twisting through spindly new growth. "Let's go back," I said. "I don't like being in the woods at night."

Eyes trained on the road's next bend, I calculated. Dylan would go to jail. That meant he wouldn't stay. Sure, he might return once he'd completed his sentence—but I didn't see it. Should I risk liking a man unbound to Zendik?

Would I slow my sexual evolution if I *didn't* risk it?

My sexual evolution—I lingered on Dylan's bond to "this girl" just long enough to dismiss it. How could lovers join in the Deathculture, split by walls of lies?

As the road curved toward the Farm, I roused my nerve and took my risk.

"Do you wanna kiss?"

"No," he said, gazing straight ahead.

I understood this no; I just didn't believe it. A couple years earlier, I'd been first to go on a walk with a shy newcomer a few years my junior. We'd hiked up to a bald hilltop with a sweeping view of the surrounding mountains. Other Zendiks called it the Landing Pad; I called it the Moon Landing. By moonlight that night, I asked if he wanted to kiss. He said no. I kissed him anyway. He kissed me back and told me later that he'd said no only out of fear that he wouldn't know what to do. At nineteen, he'd not yet kissed a girl.

Though I assumed Dylan had kissed other girls, I took his no to be negotiable also. As we ascended the driveway, as we neared the Farmhouse, as my chance began to vanish, I took another risk. I stopped, grabbed him by the shoulders, and kissed him on the mouth. He was twenty-one; I was twenty-six.

Later, by letter, he would say, *You shouldn't have done that. You betrayed my trust.* Had the shy nineteen-year-old felt the same?

Stopped in the driveway, Dylan returned my kiss, pressing against me with his lips, chest, hips. I clasped his hands and stepped back.

"Let's go to a date space. The one behind the Addition."

In the date space, we made out but didn't disrobe, so as not to cross the line from walk to date. Zendiks weren't supposed to go on dates with visitors still on quarantine.

By the next morning, the rest of the Farm knew I'd necked with Dylan. Two nights later, we had our first date. The morning after that, he came off quarantine—six days early. He knew how to cook, we needed cooks, and everyone agreed that if he had any bugs they'd already entered the communal stew through me.

Soon we, too, were sleeping together, in my bed, with Eile's blessing. *She* spent most nights in her lover's bunk in the Addition—just one flight up from Arol's kitchen.

Prying lath from studs that had once held shelves for a square couple's dishware, I heard a break in the squawk of nails, the croak of planks, next door, where the rest of my crew was removing the living room floor. Through slits between lath strips, I spied a half-dozen Zendik men, crowbars stilled on booted toes, in a ring around Dylan.

I paused to listen.

"So you got us pegged, huh? You're here, what, a week, and you're gonna give us input? Man, this ain't no rainbow-hippie tree-sit. It's a whole new way to live. You're an apprentice here, not an expert. I don't care *where* you've been."

"I was just saying that I thought maybe—"

"Go ahead, *fight* the power. *Get* arrested. But don't expect a medal. *We* know that whole scene is *bull*shit."

"That's not what—"

"Look, you gotta give it up. You gotta trust us. We're not gonna rip you off. Just relax. Let us in. We're your friends."

Dylan's shoulders slumped under his patchwork coat. He opened his mouth, then closed it. He dropped his gaze to the splintered subfloor. The ring dissolved; voices fused with the thud of crowbars.

I felt for Dylan; I knew the sting of demolition. Yet the men's attack struck me as an act of love. They'd torn him down so he could re-form, like the boards we'd haul back to the Farm, into part of something larger. And they'd sanctioned my interest in him by "giving him energy."

But no amount of pounding could beat back my mounting

anxiety over being with an outsider. I could *feel* others searching us for signs of squareness, amassing damning evidence. Any day, any minute, we would be charged.

I could wait and sweat—or turn us in and find us guilty.

I ran my verdict by the girls first. With their help, I marshaled my "I" statements—the same clichés I'd used to dump Amory. After lunch, one day past the demo, I called Dylan over to join the girls and me in a ring of chairs we'd prepared in the dining hall. He sat opposite me, in the last empty seat.

I told him it was over.

His eyes sparked. "That's fine, if *you* want to break up. I can respect that. But"—he gestured at the rest of the ring—"is this really *your* decision?"

"Yes," I said.

He yanked the band from his head, letting his curls drop to shield his eyes. With the band crushed in his fist, he shoved his chair from the ring and stalked outside.

That evening, chopping carrots for the dinner salad at a butcher block in the main kitchen, I glimpsed a misplaced flicker.

Riven had ducked into the walk-in for an onion. Eile was blending tomatillos for green sauce at one end of the long counter along the back wall. Rayel, stationed at the other end, was spooning sour cream into a serving bowl. Between them lay eight pans of enchiladas, topped with grated cheese, waiting to bake in our mammoth range. The flicker lurked beneath the pans, hidden from Rayel and Eile.

Riven emerged from the walk-in and caught it.

"Rayel! Eile! Fire!"

Rayel and Eile jumped back from the counter. Tomatillo pulp blurped out of Eile's blender. Rayel's spoon hit the flagstone floor.

A tongue of flame shot past the enchiladas.

Rayel gasped. I shrieked. Eile scrambled down the steps to the sinks and out the side door. Rayel and Riven dashed out the back. The flame exploded into a sheet of raging orange, leaping to meet the cathedral ceiling and drowning the sound of voices in its roar. A thick smoke pillow filled the kitchen. Crouched to stay under it, I ran for the pantry.

In the chill air, in the clear dark, I once again heard voices.

"Extinguishers! Get the rest!"

"Where?"

"Check the Potato Shed!"

"Already checked!"

"Get the long hose from the garden!"

"It's right here!"

"More buckets!"

"I'll get 'em!"

"Pots! Fill pots!"

"No! Don't go in the kitchen!"

Chances to help lit up and winked out. I hovered, inert, knowing Zendiks didn't idle in crisis yet daring, since night hid me, to dodge the chaos.

Ladders clattered into position against the back wall of the kitchen. Boots thudded past me. Goose bumps roughened my skin.

"Kitchen's clear! Do a chain from the sinks!"

A chain. I can do a chain.

I stepped inside.

Soot blackened every surface in the kitchen and grayed the dining-hall ceiling and walls. Dinner was charcoal. I grabbed a soup pot from under one of the butcher blocks and descended to the dish pit.

In less than fifteen minutes, the fire had been all but extinguished, and the building saved from structural harm. Only a swath of siding, just under the roof, still burned. I filled pots as a couple guys on extension ladders doused the last of the flames, at the top of the chain. Cool gusts rushed in through the back door like group sighs of relief.

Yet *my* relief was incomplete.

Filling pots, I glimpsed Dylan at the next sink. Guilt stiffened my shoulders and closed my throat. He—the lingering charge between us—must have triggered my paralysis.

What kind of warrior *was* I? What kind of weapon? I'd let some dumb crush stun me, with a battle on.

Would Arol intuit my failure? Pass it over? What would she reveal had caused the fire?

The last flame snuffed, all of us thrust into her kitchen in a seething, red-cheeked swarm, crowding the doorways and packing the floor. More than forty Zendiks thronged a room meant for five or ten.

Arol, seated with her back against the table, commanded a pocket of calm. She sipped chamomile tea as we squeezed into a breathless equilibrium. Setting her mug down, she addressed my burning question.

"I'm trying to figure this fire out, what it means psychically. And what's coming to me is that the world doesn't want us to have nice things. To them, our kitchen–dining hall is a threat. It's too glamorous. It shows we're not just a bunch of hippies shitting in the woods."

Few outsiders would have called our kitchen–dining hall "glamorous." It was neither sleek nor shiny. It didn't stink of money. Instead, it testified to thousands of hours of labor: by hand, we'd laid the foundation, raised walls of mortar and cordwood, leveled a flagstone mosaic on a shifting bed of sand.

"And *we're* not sure we deserve nice things either. We're afraid to take our place as a successful, aesthetically advanced artistic movement. So the fire was a test. And you guys passed it. It was incredible how everybody pulled together."

That can't be it, I thought.

She hadn't mentioned sex.

In every other tale she'd told of flames, sex was to blame.

For example: Years earlier, a candle had tipped onto her pillow and torched a house, one night when she was set to get together with someone else and Wulf was jealous. Had they faced this tension and joined to fight it, her pillow would not have ignited.

Forty-eight hours later, shredding lettuce for dinner in the Farmhouse kitchen, I spotted Arol by the living room doorway, giving an order to one of the men: "Get everybody in here. *Now.*"

Fear reared in my throat, plunged through my gut, pooled in my bladder. Just as it had before my father's spankings. Just as it had when the man in the dark coat, deep underground, had advanced to attack me.

Ten minutes later, to a packed living room, Arol delivered the verdict I'd been waiting for.

"The fire," she hissed, skin taut across her cheekbones, "has nothing to do with the world. It's about all of *you* and your stupid, square relationships. All sleeping together—everybody in a couple—and I didn't even *know*. *Swan* had to tell me. How *dare* you?"

Her gaze swept the forest of upturned faces, raising a guilty flush on each it touched. Though *my* guilt had already consumed my fling with Dylan, I, too, blazed with the common shame.

"You guys disgust me. If this is how you wanna be, you can all leave. I'll take Swan and the kids and get an apartment. I'll do this revolution by myself. I'm through with your bullshit. I'm *through* with it."

That night, each sack in the Potato Shed held one Zendik. By the time we'd wiped the last patch of soot from the walls, most couples had dissolved.

Alone again, we could love Arol best. *She* would be our only flame.

[chapter 11]

Arol's Embrace

I STOOD BESIDE KRO IN THE palm of our Farm, night hiding us from other humans. It was 5:00 a.m., a month past the fire and three years after I'd had sex for the first time, with him as my guide, beneath a quilt in this same field. I'd pulled him from the trailer, hours into a marathon date, to offer him a song. This was risky. Singing exposed me. So far, as a Zendik, I'd sung only on solo hikes down sleeping roads.

Kro reached under my blouse to caress my waist. Dew crept through the hems of my long black pants. We faced north, toward the pond and woods, where the wild creatures met their own needs, mated as they pleased. Across the creek, to the east, the bucks paced their pen, snorting and grunting, awaiting the day when the does would go into heat and Arol would choose who would sire that year's batch of kids.

Kro's hand dropped back to his thigh. I closed my eyes, raised my chin, and poured out a folk ballad I'd carried with me since college—one of just a few songs strong enough to survive my story that only Zendik music was pure. Imitating Joan

Baez, I stretched the final syllable of each line of the refrain into its own prolonged lament:

> *She walks these hills in a long black ve-e-e-e-eil*
> *Visits my grave when the night winds wa-a-a-a-ail*
> *Nobody kno-o-ows*
> *Nobody see-ee-ees*
> *Nobody knows but me-e-e*

In the song, a man cuckolds a friend and dies by the rope. Yet all I heard as I sang was the lyrics' grace and flow. My own betrayal—my journey west—had morphed into a quest for certainty: that I would die a Zendik and be with Kro. Maybe someday we'd have babies together. If I could trust him with my singing, I thought, I could trust him with anything.

But I still craved dates with other men.

In particular, I craved a date with Mason.

I'd spoken with him by phone around the time of the fire, when he'd yet to leave Ohio. Nothing was keeping him from moving in with us, he'd said—except student debt.

I'd advised default. A collection agency would buy his loans from the government and try to track him down. If they found him, they'd call and run their playbook: threat, compromise, guilt trip. Once they saw he had no income, they'd give up.

Weeding strawberries with him one late-April morning, on a slope overlooking the creek, I learned that he had indeed defaulted, that he'd lasted a scant six months at the job he'd quit to come to Zendik, that no strand of romance tied him back home.

His thread to the Deathculture was frayed enough that he might stay.

Where Kro was ox-strong—hard to budge, mighty once in motion—Mason was antelope-fleet: all vigor and sinew, poised to spring up and gallop. He leaped to the running-around jobs, the fetching-and-carrying jobs, the sweating-and-gasping jobs that Kro would only do if Arol said he had to. Feeling my own lethargy, when it rose, as a sinister undertow, I stretched toward those who seemed to surf above its current, doubt a mere cirrus wisp in their distance. Naked in a date space with Mason, I imagined, I might drink in some of his vim—then return, thirst quenched, to Kro.

Hadn't Wulf and Arol "balled around"? Hadn't polyamory paired with honesty begotten the union at the heart of our revolution?

Maybe so. But that didn't pacify Kro. When I told him I hoped to go on a date with Mason, he slipped into livid silence. I bolted. As if I could avoid him in a world as small as ours.

He charged me one gray May morning, on a garden crew, as I forced a cartload of wet compost over sodden ground. Our eyes hadn't met in days. He stopped my cart. Our eyes collided.

"I don't see how we can be together. We can't even talk to each other. I'm done. Unless *you* have a solution."

Feeling my load sink in the mud, dreading the shove it would take to get it going again, I shook my head. Tears blurred my vision. Drizzle seeped from the haze veiling the garden. Neither source of moisture could dissolve the block between us. I had no solution.

That evening after milking, trudging down the hill from the goat barn, I crushed thoughts of Kro. His steady warmth. His creosote kiss. His gleeful grin.

I missed him.

I also missed Arol, on her knees, weeding the flower bed fronting the Farmhouse.

"How are you doing, Helen?" she called.

I started. Any other day, I would have seen her first.

I stepped over to the rail between path and bed and clutched the rough wood. She smiled up at me, eyes bright. The whale on her cheek crested and fell. Around her, snapdragons blazed in shades of red and purple. Come midsummer, there'd be cosmos, rudbeckia, sunflowers, echinacea. This bed, like the others Arol tended, was a four-dimensional painting whose colors and composition shifted with her whims and the seasons.

"Not so good," I said. "I'm pretty bummed about it being over between me and Kro."

"Why does it have to be over?" She set her trowel down and straightened her back. "Is that what *you* want?"

"No!" My voice broke. Fresh tears wet my cheeks. "I feel like I really love him. I mean, yeah, I have other attractions— but *he's* the one I wanna *be* with."

She tucked a hank of hair behind her ear and nodded sympathetically. "The problem I see in your relationship with Kro is that you don't get help from anyone close in who's made a relationship work. You talk to these other guys who are just as lost as you are. The blind leading the blind, you know? *They* don't know how to do it either!"

Leaning forward again, she gouged out a snarl of bindweed and periwinkle. "*I'd* be willing to help you guys with your relationship," she said, tossing the weeds on her waste pile, "if you wanna try again."

My tears slowed. I noticed the persimmon trees across the path, glowing with new growth. Breathing deeply for the first time in days, I drank in the moist fertility of the world budding around me. Snapdragons fluttered like tiny flags in the heart's army.

"I do! I want to!"

"Is Kro around? Why don't you go get him and we'll see if he's into it?"

I dashed up to Kro's space, on the second floor of the Farmhouse. He was stretched on his bed, eyes closed, arms folded over his chest, ears cased in headphones. *How does he get away with lying around, listening to music, when it's not even dark out? Oh, yes—that threatening gaze.*

Alerted by the creak of floorboards under my feet, he opened his eyes and removed an earpiece, raising an eyebrow in inquiry.

"Arol wants to talk to you," I said, knowing that invoking her name was the quickest way to set my beloved ox in motion. Outside, I resumed my post at the rail. Kro stood a few yards away. Stealing glances at him as he listened to Arol repeat her take on our failure, I thought I saw his shoulders drop, his spine straighten.

Arol jabbed the ground at the edge of a clump of spiky grass, tugging it with her free hand. I saw a band of matted root, still clutching subsoil. The clump wasn't ready to come out yet. She let it drop. She looked from Kro to me and back to Kro. "You guys could be the model Zendik couple," she said, her eyes steady on his. "You just have to communicate. You have to commit to asking me for help when you hit a rough spot. You wanna try it?"

His jaw loosened. His brow lifted. A grin budded from his lips and bloomed to fill his face. "Yeah," he said. "I do."

In a trice I was at his side. He crooked his arm around my shoulder; I curled mine around his waist and looked up at him, mirroring his grin.

Arol stood and traded her trowel for a spading fork. She stamped the tines in to the hilt, along a fresh edge of the stubborn clump. Yanking the fork back, she pulled it up, then kicked it into its rut, upside down, so it would die for lack of light. Still snug against Kro, I caught her eye.

"Thank you, Arol," I said.

A few days later, the lingering trouble of my crush on Mason drove me to the Addition to ask Arol's help.

That morning, to boost my courage, I'd donned my most flattering shirt—mint green, with pearly snaps—and my best pair of jeans. I'd dabbed rose oil on my wrists, neck, armpits. I'd washed my hair and combed it into a long ponytail. My nails—thanks to an hour spent scrubbing lunch dishes—were clean.

On the steps to the front entrance, I paused to listen. All I heard was the kids' clamor, mixed with Swan's murmur, coming from the Treehouse. That relieved me. If Arol was in her kitchen, she didn't have company.

I stopped again on the top step, hand on the knob. Could I do this? Did I dare? I reminded myself that Arol had *ordered* me to come around when Kro and I floundered. Hanging back posed the greater risk.

I turned the knob and pushed the door open. Closing it behind me, I caught the plunk of teacup against tabletop. Still no voices. Blood rushed to my cheeks. I turned down the hall, hot with fear and excitement.

The kitchen door stood ajar. I knocked—not too softly, not too hard.

"Come in!"

Arol sat at her table, facing me, a finger curled through the grip of her cup. Behind her, linden branches nuzzled the window screen. Above the window, a half-dozen wide-mouthed jars, filled with beans and grains, lined a smooth pine shelf.

"I came because I need help with Kro."

She waved me to take a seat. Sliding into one of her four matching chairs, I felt my heartbeat slow almost to normal. The hardest part—the approach—was over.

"It's great being back together with Kro, but I just can't get this new guy, Mason, off my mind. I feel like I *have* to know what it's like to touch him. Like I'll be missing something big if I don't." Beneath the certainty I thought I'd found lurked doubt I couldn't think about: What if my "out" *hadn't* shown me to my mate? What if Kro *wasn't* the one?

As I blurted, Arol nodded, looking both girlish and maternal with her hair in two braids, streaked white and gray.

I trusted her to tame the snarl between Kro and me, weave it into neat plaits.

She rested her chin in her palm and pressed a fingertip against the whale's tail. Shifting forward, she gazed at me, eyes narrowed, as if divining her reply from signs in my irises. Steam wafted up from her teacup. Lavender scent seeped in from the terrace. The refrigerator purred. Set against the main kitchen's cavernous walk-in, with its bank of roaring fans, this fridge—spotless, white, single family–size—struck me as a small miracle of calm. Even as my mind raced to guess what Arol might say, I basked in the closeness of our moment alone.

She lifted her chin from her palm and tugged at the tuft of one braid. "Kro wants to have dates with other people, right? He likes to make it with Shure, Rayel, Riven every now and then."

I nodded.

The flat of her hand hit the tabletop with a soft thwack. "If he wants to ball around, it has to work both ways. He can't get pissed at you for doing it, too."

I nodded again, pleased I'd won tacit permission to hit on Mason.

"And on your end, you've gotta communicate with Kro. He's your top priority. You wanna make it with someone else, you tell him first. Some other guy might drive your box wild, but he's the one you're with."

On my date with Mason, the earth did not shake. So I homed back to Kro, still certain on the surface, to lift his brow with forgive-me kisses.

We both knew he *had* to take me back, since I'd strayed with Arol's leave.

I was hunting fresh events for the summer selling calendar, at one of the Addition computers, when Arol's question floated down from above:

"Wouldn't it be great to have little mulatto babies running around?"

The word "mulatto" caught my ear—a word I'd read in books but wasn't used to hearing. *What's she talking about? Is she talking to* me?

I looked up. Arol was leaning over the rail of the staircase spiraling down to the main office from the loft, where Kro, in headphones, was working at his desk. She fixed me with an impish grin.

"Don't you get the best genes when you mix the races?"

She *was* talking to me. She was suggesting that Kro and I get pregnant.

Little mulatto babies. I was twenty-six and a half in June 2003. I'd long thought that if I gave birth I'd wait till my thirties. My mother had borne her first child at thirty and her last (me) at thirty-four. Arol had birthed Swan at thirty-seven. Rayel— the only Zendik woman besides Swan to give birth since my arrival—had done so at thirty-two, after almost a decade and a half at Zendik. I'd assumed that earning leave to breed would take at least a few more years. But as Arol beamed down on me, I conceived a new story, starring mocha-skinned toddlers who romped up the steps to hug her knees, their squeals, sharp and excited, announcing my place in the family of Zendiks. They'd bind me for life to Kro (marriage was a sham; we'd never get married) and, even better, to Arol—their grandmother. If there was a way to forge the ties of a natural-born Zendik, this, I thought, was it.

Little mulatto babies. Of *course* Kro would accept Arol's proposal, if I did. Didn't every man lust to spread his seed? It wasn't as if he'd be signing on as sole breadwinner for a nuclear family, or even Mr. Mom. Zendik children mostly stuck together, in the care of their mothers and other women, with Zar's Australian shepherd, Apache, standing guard. Fatherhood would not force a drastic shift in how Kro spent his time.

Little mulatto babies. Arol, who was Jewish, had married a Catholic as a teenager and given birth for the first time at seventeen. Then, taking her infant son, she fled her husband's beatings. Working as a secretary in New York City, she fought to make ends meet.

She couldn't. So she called a family meeting and asked each relative to help her out with a monthly pledge. They, in turn, urged her to visit a woman named Yeti, at Jewish Family Services. "Yeti will help you," they said.

Arol thought Yeti would connect her with the money she'd asked of her family. Instead, Yeti suggested that she pass her son to a nice, well-to-do Jewish couple who'd raise him in a stable home and pay for college. Arol felt betrayed, but she agreed. Her son was two when she gave him up.

Her surrender left her shattered. She broke down, slept around, wound up in the gutter. Some friends, seeing she was courting early death, got her drunk (to calm her fear of flight) and packed her off to San Francisco. The change of scene could not heal the wound of losing her child, but it did revive her. By the time she met Wulf in Los Angeles, a couple years later, she'd pulled herself together.

This story of Arol's son—passed to me by one of her confidants—did not serve the Farm's creation myth. So I never heard it, as a Zendik. Instead, watching her lurking hurt reverberate through Rayel's first years of motherhood, I assumed that Rayel, playing out a Deathculture script, had brought her pain on herself.

By the time Rayel gave birth, in 2001, she'd seen Arol separate a number of mothers from their babies. Arol would convict the mother of bad mothering, then turn the child over to other Zendiks, usually for one or more stretches of multiple months. Rayel had delayed getting pregnant in part because she'd feared such treatment (which Swan alone had escaped). Choosing to risk childbearing, she'd let herself hope the pattern would break.

It didn't. After bombarding her with charge after charge, Arol forbade Rayel to care for her infant. In the two months they were apart, Rayel sank into desolation so deep that Arol assigned her the therapeutic task of weaving baskets.

I could have gathered, from watching Rayel, that Zendik motherhood was a cliff to be approached with caution, if at all. Instead, riding high on Arol's approval, I let my A-student arrogance prevail. Hadn't I won the highest grades in the history of Dominican Academy? Hadn't I been the first of its graduates to spend every single quarter on the Principal's List? As in high school, I thought, so in child rearing: I would succeed where others had failed, because I was smarter and I would work harder.

I grinned back at Arol, bursting with pride and excitement.

"Yeah," I said. "It would be wild to try to have kids."

Arol waved to Kro to take off his headphones and come to the top of the stairs. He nodded at her, descended a few steps, nodded at me.

"What do you think of being a father?" she asked.

Kro backed into the railing and scrunched his nose into his eyebrows, as if working to merge what he'd just heard with life as he'd known it a moment ago.

"Let me get this straight," he said, staring down at me. "*You* wanna have a *ba*by?"

Maybe Kro knew, better than I did, how little my desire to have a baby had to do with having a baby.

"Yes. I do. I mean, I don't know if it'll happen, but I at least wanna try."

He shook his head and shrugged. Arol and I had already hatched a plan. He could resist—or give in.

He glanced at Arol, then back at me, with a tiny, puzzled smile. "Okay," he said, shifting his gaze between us. "If that's what you want, I guess I'll go along with it."

In Arol's embrace I felt I'd gained a great height—a subpeak, at least, in my climb to enlightenment. From here I saw further than my peers. This, it seemed, qualified me to steer them past snags in their lives.

One midsummer afternoon, I glimpsed a chance to inflict guidance.

I was in the Addition kitchen, winding down a counseling session, when Ethik—one of Swan's ex-boyfriends and the Farm's head carpenter—dropped in for a drink of water. Arol asked him how it was going with Eile. They'd had a few dates, in the past month.

Ethik sank into a seat at the table. "I like getting together with her," he said, "but whenever we make contact outside of that, she acts all skittish, like a spooked horse. I can't get her to calm down."

Arol nodded. "Yeah, I've seen her get like that, too. She needs some kind of therapy. Something to ground her."

I knew what Ethik and Arol were talking about. That summer I'd noticed a high, tinny tone to Eile's laughter, a manic insistence on staying in motion. None of us linked her agitation to the break she'd recently been forced to make with Lysis, her longtime boyfriend. Had it come up, we would have dismissed it. They'd *needed* to separate. The fever between them had threatened their ardor for Zendik.

In addition to Ethik, a number of other men had hit Eile up for dates since her breakup. Often she said no. Sometimes her suitors waited a week or two and tried again. Maybe they were thick, or hard up for targets; maybe she hinted there was hope. In my story, warped by envy, she was enacting a plan to string men along: flirt, reject, flirt some more, reject again. *I'd* always wished to be the Girl With the Most Hit-Ups, not the Girl Most Likely to Hit Up the Guy Herself. Clearly, the swirl of pursuit around Eile was fucking her up.

As I listened to Ethik and Arol dissect Eile, I twisted my

take on her state into a cure. Then, with Arol's permission, I delivered my diagnosis—and my prescription: "I say, guys stop hitting her up. *She* has to hit on a different guy each week. That way, she can't hook anyone into hoping she's gonna say yes next time, or be his girlfriend."

Arol nodded. "Sounds good to me. Why don't you go let her know? You can keep an eye on her to make sure she follows through."

With that, I became Eile's warden.

Sometimes captives strike back.

The first mark Eile chose was Kro.

When he agreed to a date with her, I feigned indifference—recalling, with relief, that she'd have to try someone new the next week.

For a month or so, Eile followed her program. Had it calmed her? I couldn't tell. I *did* sense rising hostility in her vibe toward me—a healthy defense against being treated with arrogance for an illusory disease. I retaliated by complaining to Arol, who sustained my plea to drop responsibility for Eile's therapy. "I'm not gonna try to help someone who doesn't wanna be helped," I declared to the group at lunch one afternoon. "I don't deserve that kind of anger coming at me."

In *my* mind, I'd done my best to save Eile—and she'd resolved to stay lost. Whatever followed was her own fault.

A week later, at lunch, Eile dropped, flushed and breathless, into the seat next to me. I was clustered with most of the other girls at one end of the long table dominating the dining hall. She seemed tightly wound yet somehow grounded, as if her manic electricity had found a central meridian.

"You guys, I've decided. I'm going out."

What? No one spoke. She hurried on. "I feel like I still have fantasies to deal with. Like dancing out in the world. And marrying a rich guy who'll take care of me."

Eile had danced before Zendik. She'd even moved to New

York City to test her chances of dancing professionally. At the Farm, she'd danced with Swan, but always in supporting roles, and for long stretches she hadn't danced at all. She may have known, deep down, that if she couldn't dance, she couldn't be part of our revolution.

The rich husband? Maybe he played the same role for Eile that rape played for me. Had Zendik taught her she wanted him, even as it warned her the want was corrupt and could be crushed only through suffering?

The other girls—Karma, Cayta, Mar, Riven—peppered her with variations on the same cautions I'd heard a year earlier, before I'd left for Idaho: "Hang in—you'll get through this." "Can't you work out your fantasies in your head?" "People don't change when they go out; they just get more desperate." "Why do you want more of the same old pain?"

None of them had ever gone "out."

I said nothing till they left the table. Then I turned to Eile. Her face was still flushed; her breathing had calmed. "I don't think it's wrong to go out," I said. "Sometimes you have to hit bottom to feel what you really want." I described my civil war of the previous summer—how I'd *wanted* to want to come back to Zendik all along but hadn't *actually* wanted to till after Alvin's assault. Facing him—in the myth I'd spun since then—had both spurred my return and firmed my resolve. Maybe the plunge Eile was about to take would raise her, someday, to a perch as high as mine.

The next morning, Kro and I happened to be on the porch roof of the Farmhouse, priming a section of second-floor siding for a coat of sunflower yellow, when Eile's mother inched her station wagon down from the dining hall and stopped at the top of the driveway. The backseat was crammed with Eile's stuff. The passenger seat was empty. Maybe Eile was doing a final sweep of her space or saying a last goodbye. Just as she reached the car and grabbed the door pull, Kro caught my eye and waved his paintbrush at the boom box he'd set on a windowsill. The song "Mother and Child Reunion," from the album *Paul Simon*, was playing.

"Get it?" he said. "The mother and child reunion?"

"Yeah." I returned his smirk. "It's a motion away."

Below us, the station wagon descended the drive. I gazed out over the fields and woods sloping toward the road, my view stretching far beyond Eile's. It would stretch farther still as my ascent continued.

Yet I couldn't relax and enjoy the panorama. With each step up, I breathed thinner air, risked more if I slipped.

My only safety was Arol's grip.

On September 27, 2003—while I was still trying to make "little mulatto babies" with Kro—I told Arol at her kitchen table that I wished to hit on Zar.

And Prophet.

My cheeks burned as I said the second name. No one—*no one*—hit on Prophet. Merely flashing on the option, the previous fall at Voodoo Fest, after imagining Arol might die, had gravely aggravated my original thought crime.

But I'd come to trust, over months in her favor, that nothing I said could rock her. That her vast view compassed much that would have shocked the less evolved.

Arol sipped her tea. "Why do you want to hit on them?"

Why indeed? I saw them as ascended beings, rendered reachable—maybe—by my recent rise. Tasting their sexual superpowers would speed my climb. And—who knew?—a surprise eruption of dormant attraction might yet rocket me to the top tier of the Zendik pyramid.

I *had* to make this bid—despite my story assuring me I'd grow old with Kro.

"I'm curious about what it's like to get together with them."

"That's odd," she said, chin level, gaze steady. "If you're curious about how they are sexually, wouldn't it be easier just to ask someone who's fucked them?"

"I guess it's more than curiosity. I want the *experience*."

She glanced into her teacup, then back at me. "I can tell you about Zar—of course it's been a long time—and I can definitely tell you about Prophet."

She seemed not to have heard that I sought more than an oral report. But I wasn't about to refuse juicy gossip. I leaned in to listen.

Arol said that Zar loved messing around, pushing boundaries. This jibed with another woman's rave review of how he'd fucked her while probing her ass with his finger. Prophet, Arol said, wasn't much for foreplay—he skipped straight to sex. "He's an artist, you know?" She laughed. "Artists are like that. They know what they want and go for it. You've probably had the same experience with Kro."

I nodded, despite a blip of dissonance. Kro reveled in foreplay.

She studied me for a long moment. Her speech had not cooled my cheeks. "You still want to hit on them, don't you? Getting the rundown isn't enough."

I nodded again.

She shrugged. "You can go ahead and hit on Prophet. I doubt he'll say yes—he's a one-woman kind of guy—but I don't mind if you try."

Prophet painted and sculpted in a spacious studio built to suit him. He drummed in the band. He assembled collections of Wulf's writings and collaborated with Lysis to design the magazine. He did not sell. He did not cook or help clean the main kitchen. He did not receive group input. I would never see him crumple in shame as the rest of us struck him with pebbles of blame.

These perks did not come cheap. He knew the terms of his trade.

She sat back and folded her arms across her chest. "The sooner the better, I guess. As long as you're in fantasy about these other guys, you don't have a relationship with Kro."

She half-smiled at me, a hint of conspiracy in her up-twisted lip. "Sounds like you have some hitting up to do."

I found Zar in his recording studio in the Mobile, enthroned before his massive console, mixing Arol's latest album, *Into the Oracle*. Hovering just inside the doorway, I stuttered out my hit-up. After a short pause, he swiveled toward me.

"I guess I'd be into it. But not tonight."

Prophet, at his desk in the Treehouse, stroked his goatee. A power surge through his hard drive flickered its lime light. Excitement and dread—*what if he says yes?*—warred in my chest.

"I'm flattered you asked me—but no," he said.

The next day, when Zar switched his yes to no, I was more relieved than disappointed. I'd tried climbing higher by taking other lovers. Now I could fall back to Kro.

Any other year, I would have been thrilled to sell the KROQ Weenie Roast at the Verizon Wireless Amphitheatre in Charlotte, North Carolina. "Power" sellers had been known to make five to eight hundred dollars each at the all-day Ozzfest knock-off; being chosen to go was a vote of confidence. But on Sunday, October 5, 2003, I—like most of my seven-woman crew—was fighting fatigue and a hangover. We would have been glad to stay home.

Saturday night we'd gotten drunk and lost sleep at a rare Farm-wide alcohol party. I'd made the mistake of staying up till three, after pulling Kro away from the dining hall for an impromptu date. Worse, I'd spent part of the date having Kro play oracle. Raising questions about the fates of various Zendiks—Would this one leave the Farm? Would this one?—I'd insisted that he answer yes or no, without thinking. Worst of all, I couldn't shake a hunch that Rayel—a crewmate who Kro had said would leave—was about to betray us.

Was this a thought crime I ought to confess?

Was I wrongfully condemning Rayel to soul death?

Or was it a psychic nudge?

If it was and I let her wreck our trip, I'd be liable. If it was and I spoke up, I'd climb a little higher.

By midday, I was low on cash and craving a breakthrough. Dazed and sunburned, I scanned the food court for tie-dye, dreadlocks, dime-size lobe holes, thick zippers slashing black leather. I replaced the sweat-stained magazine in my hand with a fresh one from my pants pocket. I flashed a STOP BITCHING START A REVOLUTION sticker at a man in a West Coast Choppers jacket. He smirked through his shades and kept walking. I didn't chase after him.

Tarrow strolled over, then Leah, the sole power seller on our trip. Even she was dragging. Her eyelids drooped under blotched eye shadow. The double-XL T-shirt hooked to her belt loop brushed the ground.

One by one, three more sellers drifted toward us. A huddle formed. No one—except maybe Toba, who was roaming the lawn—felt like selling. No one was doing well.

Was it Rayel's fault? Was it her vibe? Or was I dulling us with my thought crime? She was right there in the huddle. If I spoke now, I'd at least close the question of whether to speak.

"Hey, guys? I wanna say something. I bet it's bullshit, but I feel like if I don't say it I won't be able to sell."

Five pairs of eyes widened. Five heads nodded. Five necks stretched my way.

"I was up super late with Kro last night, and we were playing this game where I asked him questions and he gave the first answer that came to him. One thing I asked was if Rayel was gonna leave. He said yes." I glanced at Rayel, then glanced away. "Now I can't get it out of my head that Rayel's on her way out."

Five heads swiveled toward Rayel. Her face fell. My heart sank. I knew how it felt to be singled out for doubt.

She took a quick step back, shrinking from attack. "Maybe you're sensing some kind of weakness in me. I know I'm not as strong as I could be. But I'm *definitely* not planning to *leave*."

I apologized, assuring her I hadn't *bought* my story; I'd just had to tell it so I could sell. Everyone seemed to accept this. Yet I didn't sell any better the rest of the day, and neither did anyone else. Each of us totaled two to three hundred—far less than we'd hoped.

I knew Arol and Swan would hate how little we'd made. But, I thought, the drubbing I was in for wouldn't crush me— all seven of us would share the blame.

The next morning, gathered at the dining hall table with every adult Zendik except Arol and Prophet, I learned I'd mis-led myself: I alone was going to pay.

The table, built to seat all forty of us, with room to spare, was a heavy wooden parenthesis with a cat-pupil slit down the middle. I called it the Eye of Sauron table because this slit mimicked the void, irised by fire, through which Tolkien's formless villain keeps watch over his kingdom and those who wear his rings.

Swan, at the table's head, stretched forward and pressed fingers crowned with polished nails into its glossy finish. Jaw clenched, she addressed us.

"This meeting is about Helen and the utter bullshit she pulled in Charlotte. We lost thousands of dollars because of what she did, trying to take Rayel down. Why no one had the balls to call home and turn her in—or boot her off the trip—I don't know. But the bottom line is, we can't have people betray-ing us from the inside."

The collective gaze swept to me. My eyes popped wide open, as if someone had duct-taped my lids to my cheeks and brows. *I will take this*, I thought. *I will look straight at what I did. I will not look away.*

Seconds later, Arol appeared at the top of the stairs to the kitchen, Prophet at her shoulder. Every head swiveled toward her. "It's her relationship with Kro. They're smug and superior. You all leave them alone 'cause you see them talking to me. That's not enough. They have to open their affair to the group. They can't keep running their own show."

With that, Arol let go. Of me, of my union with Kro.

Years earlier I'd written of Zendik, "There is no illusion here of unconditional love. No bond not dissoluble, in a culture based on survival."

Survival of what? Of all life, I would have said. Of our outlaw tribe. But really it was Arol's rule that fed on dissolution. For it to last, each of us had to love her best and stay possessed by how to please her. Stretches in her shitter upped our desire to suffer for her favor.

I may have hastened my fall by assailing Rayel and hitting on Prophet. I could not have stopped it.

I could have tried to flee with Kro.

I could have crept up to his space, late one night, roused him with a touch, crouched by his pillow to whisper, "Kro, I want to be with you. That can't happen here. Let's leave. Now. Let's just go."

I could have left alone, hoping he would follow.

I could have formed a scheme to lure him out.

But I wouldn't buck Arol for Kro. Or babies. Two months after the Weenie Roast, we broke for good.

Arol hadn't taken a hammer to our relationship. She'd just dropped it—not looking down—from a cliff littered at the base with shattered remains.

By December 2003, I was mourning my story of love enduring with Arol's support. If I couldn't swing this with Kro, I thought, I couldn't swing it at all.

What was left? Service to Zendik. From then on, I vowed, I'd surrender any love I found the moment a clash rose between union and group.

The day after my break with Kro, Arol approached me in the dining hall and addressed me kindly for the first time since the morning before the Weenie Roast. "You look so much better," she said. "So much more relaxed. I think you made the right choice."

I nodded, grateful for her imprimatur. Maybe, soon, I'd write something she'd want for the magazine. Maybe I'd do better on the street. Surely the circle-Z around my neck was the only ring I'd ever need.

"Thank you, Arol," I said.

[chapter 12]

Crazing

ZAR'S PICKUP TORE DOWN Regan Jackson, bed crammed with fifteen Zendiks. I stood behind the cab, clutching the front crossbar of the truck's rack, hair rough with dust. The morning sun warming my skin warned of a sweaty day to come.

As Zar hung a right onto Deep Gap, I craned my neck for a longer look at a green velvet dell enveloping a stone-rimmed pond that belonged in a fairy tale. Past the pond lay a meadow edged by a stream—and pimpled with a grid of range poles. Wildcat Spur had been sold, and the new owners meant to stud the ridge with houses and reduce the meadow to a hole on a golf course. Every day, flatbed semis packed with tree trunks thundered down the mountain.

The seller, George Levin—described to me when I'd arrived in 1999 as "some rich jerk from Florida"—had realized a hefty profit, thanks to soaring demand for housing in and around Asheville. His greed, Arol said, was bleeding our ecosphere. She'd decided to move the entire Farm, animals and all, to West Virginia. Having fled first San Diego's and then

Austin's boomtown sprawl, only to face the metastasis of Asheville, she sought respite in a backward state with a shrinking population. Plus, West Virginia was hours closer than North Carolina to markets like Boston, New York, and Washington, with their perpetual flows of fresh prospects.

Within West Virginia, Arol chose Pocahontas County, which had drawn waves of back-to-the-landers decades earlier. More than half the county's acreage was preserved in the public trust, and its air, water, and soil were some of the state's purest. By late July 2004, she'd purchased a 183-acre ranch backed up against the Monongahela National Forest. It came with barns, a mansion, a stone-rimmed pond—and an $850,000 price tag. Later that summer, the North Carolina Farm, split into fourteen lots and auctioned off, would net Arol roughly $700,000, more than doubling what she'd paid in 1999. She, too, would gain from Asheville's boom.

The suggestion of West Virginia had come from Levin's caretaker, David Gillespie, who was also thinking of relocating. It was Gillespie who'd traded Arol occasional use of his excavator for thousands of hours of Zendik sweat: Zar dug a swimming hole and septic trench with Gillespie's giant iron claw; crews of six, twelve, twenty Zendiks built him an extensive cattle fence. Despite Gillespie's link to the enemy, Arol billed him as a friend.

Passing the last of the range poles, Zar swerved into an oval driveway and stopped short before a hunting lodge cum palace. I jumped down from the truck bed, brushed the dust from my hair, and stared. The house seemed large for a bachelor caretaker. Our mission, as I understood it, was to help Gillespie pack for his move off the mountain.

Zar reversed and roared off, yelling he'd return for us at lunchtime. I followed the others through a side entrance policed by a pinched man with pale, indoor skin. "Watch the carpet!" he barked. "Wipe your feet!"

He said his name was Andy, then skipped to giving orders without asking *our* names. "I want the men to wrap the heavy stuff." He pointed to a room full of desks, tables, and dressers. "And I want you girls on chairs and mirrors." He led us into a high-ceilinged parlor holding multiple sets of matching chairs and a dozen gilt-edged mirrors.

I kept my gaze blank till Andy pranced out. Then, turning to a mirror propped against the back wall, I let a sneer curl my nose and lips. "I want you girls on chairs and mirrors," I muttered, pitching my voice higher and harsher than his. *Who is this guy? Where does he get off bossing us? And what's up with giving the girls the light stuff? What are we, a bunch of fucking debutantes?*

I might have spoken up—but Arol had sent us.

I attacked the packing job. Ripped wrap off the roll in rough swaths. Crushed corners. Slapped tape on botched seams.

What if a chair leg should—oops!—strike a mirror? I fantasized smiling at the fine mesh of cracks crazing its face.

After working for about an hour, I heard Andy take a phone call in an adjoining room. "Yes, this is Mr. Levin's assistant." Pause. "I'm getting the Deep Gap house cleared out for him right now. I fly back to Miami tomorrow."

I bent low over the seam I was taping, to hide the deep flush heating my cheeks. *No wonder this house is so huge! We are working—for free!—for the asshole who's wrecking our home.*

I wasn't the only one who'd overheard Andy's conversation. When I straightened up, Leah was squinting at me in livid disbelief.

"Did you hear that?" I whispered.

She nodded.

"What the fuck?"

She shook her head.

"Arol must have misunderstood."

"Yeah," she said. "We'll tell her at lunch."

By the time Zar honked from the driveway, we all knew

whose stuff we were packing up. The guys didn't care, but we girls were furious. Back at the Farm, we charged up to the Addition.

Arol, sipping tea at her kitchen table, nodded as we spilled our tale of insult. I kept expecting shock, anger, indignation to fracture her composure. But her gaze stayed calm, her grip firm on her cup. When we finished, she said, "I'll talk to Zar about it."

After lunch, the men returned to Deep Gap. I could not work out how this served Zendik. Arol—typically adept at stitching rips in her scrim of plausibility—had bewildered me.

Maybe she was too consumed by the move to give her weave the care it needed.

And maybe I, torn from hope for "Love" with a capital "L," felt less compelled to mend the rips myself.

My final flame at the Farm blazed just six weeks.

Adam, like Amory, had escaped the Army by purposely failing a drug test. Then, on the G.I. Bill, he'd majored in women's studies at a historically female college—which he'd quit, in late 2003, to move to Zendik. In my eyes, he was both sensitive new age guy and sexy ex-spy; I loved the hint of machismo in his voice when, echoing his Mexican father, he sweetly called me *chica*.

We started dating in late June 2004. In mid-July, when Arol announced her plan to buy the ranch in West Virginia, she cast the move as an ordeal that would break the weak. Then she zeroed in on Adam—the newest Zendik. Would he make it?

Yes, he said. He'd stick with the mission.

I wanted to trust him.

But what if he *was* weak? What if his weakness infected me, sucked me into disloyalty?

In early August, I heard he'd made only two hundred–something at a Projekt Revolution concert where the rest of his crew had averaged five. *Uh-oh.* Sure, he was new—but if he'd been *with* them he would have caught their wave and surfed it to breakthrough.

A few days later, my all-girl crew stopped over in West Virginia, en route to Vermont to sell what was being billed as the last Phish show ever. The guy sellers, between concert trips, would stop over as well. Arol was in North Carolina with everyone else.

The new Farm stretched vast and flat, against a swell of blue hills. The stone-rimmed pond, crowned with a fountain that lit up at night, outclassed the muddy hole Zar had gouged with his borrowed claw. Indoors, floods of sunlight poured into the open kitchen and adjoining dining room through a bank of floor-to-ceiling windows. The mansion's past as a comfortable home for one family teased me with hope for harmony, while its emptiness pledged a fresh start.

All of this offered but a moment's distraction from my anguish over Adam.

The morning the men arrived, I asked Noi, their leader, for a report on Adam's performance. He confirmed that Adam had been "a drag" on the trip they'd just completed. We agreed to call a meeting.

Around noon, both crews gathered in the sun-drenched dining room, our backs to the view. I did not sit by Adam.

Noi started off with an accusing confession: "On this last trip, I caught myself thinking I didn't want Adam to have *food*, he was giving so little to our crew." He blinked in shock at the cruelty of his thought. A couple of the other men nodded. "Maybe I went there in my mind because he doesn't want to be here."

The men nodded again. Noi turned to Adam and popped the question every Zendik dreaded: "Do you want to go out?"

Eyes on the floor, Adam rubbed his palms against his kneecaps. His forehead shone with sweat. "I . . . I . . . I mean, no, I don't. But I thought . . . I thought maybe I'd go hiking in the forest here for a week or two. Take some time to get my head straight."

I'd made a similar plea years earlier, in Chicago, hoping to sidestep Cayta's demand that I sell or take the bus home. By now I knew better than to request—or endorse—breaks to reflect. And I knew we couldn't have one of our number roaming the woods, smudged and confused, shedding shadows on Zendik. A dozen heads, mine among them, wagged in censure.

Taridon, battle-ready in leather chaps, flashed Adam a scorching glance. "Look, man, don't fuck around. You're in or you're out. That's it."

Adam broke. His face crumpled, as if Taridon had triggered controlled demolition. "I think I want to go," he said, tears wetting his cheeks.

The next morning he left for California, armed with his thumb and Zendik's shove-off: $21 plus a lift to Bluefield and passage to Knoxville by bus.

His leaving lightened him, which made it seem right—even as it cast me into a romantic wasteland: the remaining Zendik men were attached, unattracted, or unattractive, and our flight to the hinterlands had all but stanched the flow of new blood.

Would I ever enjoy sex again? Revel in touch?

A week later, Arol summoned the girl and guy sellers back to West Virginia—this time for an audience with her.

From an armchair commanding the living room, she addressed the dozen of us looking up to her from a half ring on the rug.

"I want you guys to know I'm sick of being treated like an authority figure. It's not who I am. It's not fair to me." Her flaming gaze swept our faces in a merciless arc. "It has to stop."

I nodded. We nodded. I searched my past for times when my peers and I, or I alone, had forced power on Arol.

No stories leaped forth to back her charge.

She pressed on.

"It's gonna be a big change, all of us under one roof. I'm gonna be seeing a lot more of you guys day-to-day, and I'm gonna be saying what I see in the moment, same as I always have with whoever's in close."

The house had four bedrooms and three baths. Arol and her intimates would sleep in beds in the second-floor master suite, which included a bathroom, while the rest of us would roll out quilts and sleeping bags each night in the living room and the other three bedrooms (all on the ground floor) and share the other two baths. Descending the stairs in the morning, Arol would enter the mesh of common spaces—kitchen, living room, dining room—at the heart of the new Farm. As in North Carolina, every season would be open season—but here, she'd have the whole herd at close range.

She leaned forward, knees propping her elbows. "I'm not sure everybody's ready for that kind of intensity. So I'm looking at renting a house in town for whoever can't handle it." She squinted at us, as if scanning for aura shifts. "What do you think? Do you want me to do that?"

I suspect that if anyone had said yes, she would have waited a day or two, then shamed the fainthearted off the Farm.

I, for one, was ready. I imagined the coming hail of input as a hard but bracing rain speeding my purification. And I dreamed that uniting under one roof would free us from the hierarchy haunting the hardscape of the Farm in North Carolina—that the quake of the move would level us, where snipping our wristbands had failed.

But not even a quake can change a story before the story is ready to change.

A few days later, as I was prepping food for yet another selling trip, Shure burst through the pantry door in North Carolina, her face flushed, her breath quick. She'd hurried over from the Addition, where she'd been on the phone with Karma, who was with Arol in West Virginia.

"Arol kicked everyone out of the kitchen. She said we're barbarians and we'll ruin it if it stays communal. Plus, she needs a calm place to make food that can heal her, 'cause food's not just food for her; it's medicine postcancer."

Guilt drew blood to my ears and cheeks. Surely I, too, had failed at kitchen care during my stints in West Virginia. Also, I grieved our loss. I'd miss those glossy cupboards and gleaming appliances. That dazzling sunshine.

Shure rushed on. "So we'll use that other kitchen—the one in the basement, where the wife used to can."

I winced. Yes, that other kitchen. The ugly stepchild. Drably clad and starved of sun. Bathed in harsh fluorescence.

"It'll work. You'll get used to it."

I nodded. Before long I'd cease to notice the windowless gloom.

I would never adjust to the pounding anxiety of tiptoeing up to what could have been a throne room. Or the dis-ease of owing deference to those above me.

At least, on occasion, I could drink.

At socials in North Carolina, we'd been free to let loose, pair off, disperse from the Farmhouse or dining hall to additional houses and outbuildings. Arol, a light drinker turned teetotaler by cancer, usually showed briefly, if at all. Drinking brought relief.

But on a Saturday night in mid-September, when we gathered under our one and only roof for two beers each, Arol surprised me by taking an armchair in the living room, at the heart of the party.

After sitting back for an hour, she demanded that we gather 'round her. A frown pinched her mouth.

"You guys don't know how to use alcohol," she said. "The reason to drink—the reason to poison your body with that shit—

is so you can ditch your inhibitions and get real. But this whole evening—and I've been listening—I have not heard even one funky, honest conversation. It's all gossip and who's fucking who, and I'm sick of it. You guys need to grow up. Get some class. Get curious about each other. Treat booze as a tool for revolution."

As she ranted on, I grew restless, and the beer lured me toward a shocking thought: *I wish she'd shut up.* Time to get real—got it. So why not release us—while we still had a buzz—to try?

I dared not voice this thought or fully own it. Yet I could not unthink it. Lurking inside me, it awaited a surrogate target.

One morning a week later, a target appeared.

In North Carolina, I'd started most days with a trip to the outhouse, followed by goat-milking or kitchen chores. I'd had my own space, with a bed and storage for my stuff. In West Virginia, I woke, stowed my bedroll in a shared closet, and ducked across the hall to stake out the bathroom in quest of a turn on the toilet. I no longer milked goats; Arol had decreed that only those who loved them should tend them, and I saw no love in my habit of yanking laggard nannies by a rope around their necks. Also, I'd recently been stripped of my kitchen duties.

That meant I had to clean—alongside the other women with nothing more pressing to do.

As part of a changing team with no set schedule, I faced daily stress over when to begin: if Arol caught me at rest after breakfast, she might charge me with sloth; if I started alone, she might curse me for escaping into work.

After washing my oatmeal bowl on Thursday, September 23, I felt my usual tension mount toward paralysis. Feigning purpose, I retreated from the living room to the basement kitchen, grabbed a glass of water, and huddled at the island. If only I could vanish for a moment. Go unseen. I stared into the water and sipped.

A mug touched down on the island's far side, steered by a pair of hands with clean fingernails, neatly filed.

I knew those fingernails.

"What's up, Hels?" Cayta chirped. In nearly five years at Zendik, I hadn't changed my name—but I was still trying.

I looked up, meaning to fake a doing-just-fine smile. My lips resisted. I shrugged and looked back down.

Unfazed, she chirped again. "What the fuck's your problem?"

I shook my head. Studied her mug. Shrank from her eyes on my skin, my skull. Cased my brain for a sound I could make. Before I found one, she broke in.

"You better get over it, whatever it is, 'cause getting pissed isn't gonna fix things and you're gonna have to take responsibility for yourself someday."

With that, she slapped her story on me—diagnosis plus prescription—without so much as pausing to check my symptoms. Rage surged in my chest. Fuck her. Fuck this stupid island. Why the fuck had I fled *here*?

I thrust my fist up and gave her the finger.

This was my first gesture of protest at Zendik. It could have triggered others.

But she, stirring cream into her tea, didn't see it.

[chapter 13]

Break

MINUTES AFTER I'D TUCKED my finger back into my fist and quit the island for the living room, Arol opened fire: "Helen's not sure she should be here," she declared to whoever could hear. "*That's* why she's so uptight."

I hadn't been eyeing the highway. But my recent selling stats, like Adam's mediocre total at Projekt Revolution, showed I'd lost heart: a few times in the past month, I'd made just $88. Maybe, sensing the cracks in my story, she'd shifted me on her balance sheet from asset to liability and chosen to purge me.

Expulsion had its benefits: a boost in pride for survivors, plus a reminder that Arol prized our service, not our selves. She would remove those who failed.

I told myself I welcomed Arol's help; with my doubt exposed, I could gouge it out. The next morning, departing the Farm with Cayta, Mar, and Toba for a new scene—Virginia Beach—I vowed to kick butt and cleanse the taint of all those eighty-eights.

On Friday evening, as dusk descended, a cop threatened to arrest me if I kept selling. I'd been caught on film breaking the law.

First I cursed myself for drawing the cop. *What the fuck's wrong with me? How'd I vibe into that?* Then I committed thought crime: *Maybe we'll all get popped and have to go home and it won't be only my fault.* Finally I shifted toward the storefronts, counting on their awnings and knots of patrons to shield me, as I stealth-sold, from the eyes fixed to every street sign.

If only I could dodge *Cayta's* eyes.

Sure enough, when she saw me, she pounced. Why hadn't I gotten "on" yet? Scrambling to hide my thought crime, I flung up a cover about feeling competitive. She shredded it. "Why don't you focus on what you *want,* instead of what's wrong with you? Can't you relax and have some fucking *fun?*"

By "what you want," she meant "your sales goals." But I drew a burst of nerve from a slant interpretation: What if, instead of fighting my defects, I embraced my pleasure drive and let it guide me?

I rushed a couple in pressed slacks and got them to stop for my pitch. "We want a revolution for a beautiful world where we're totally honest and do what we love and no one has to wreck the earth to make money."

"We, we, we!" the man said. "What about *you?* What do *you* want?"

Normally I would have repeated the same speech, swapping "I" for "we." But this time I risked honesty. "I'm sick of being afraid," I said, checking to make sure Cayta couldn't hear. "I wanna be free to think and say and do what I want without someone coming down on me."

In tandem, the man and woman pulled out their wallets and gave me twenty bucks each for a shirt.

Yes! My big break! I glowed for a moment—then resumed my slide toward another shameful total.

By 10:00 p.m., Cayta and Toba had both been popped. They got Mar to quit. I scolded myself for feeling relieved.

I knew before counting what my number would be.

I didn't dare dissent when the others agreed to move on to DC.

Saturday morning, we set up in Georgetown. Saturday night, Cayta, flanked by Mar and Toba, drove me off the street. "You can't sell like this. You're a disgrace. Go sit in the van, hang in a coffee shop, whatever. Put your stuff away."

Sunday morning, Cayta gave me a choice: sell or leave the Farm.

I couldn't sell. I knew I'd fail. And I dreaded exile. So I asked what I'd asked years earlier, in Chicago: a day alone. A day at large. A day to chase a miracle to heal my traitor's heart.

Cayta balked; home overrode her. But it didn't matter. Miracles don't appear on demand to deliver happy plot twists. They storm stories too weak to resist.

On Monday, September 27, 2004, I woke to slivers of sun on my comforter and the sound of Cayta's voice. I slept next to a shuttered window in a bedroom whose floor I shared with four others. The window—our only one—opened onto the dining room, where Arol sipped tea in the mornings and often held court. As I rolled over so I could hear better, the dread I'd gone to bed with clutched me in a suffocating hug.

Cayta was charging me with being incorrigible.

"I'm just so *mad* at her. I can't believe she's still pulling the same bullshit after all these years."

Arol thunked her mug down. "She can't go on like this. Call a meeting. Today. Maybe there's some therapy you can try. Either that or she has to leave. You guys decide."

I pulled the comforter over my head. Feigning sleep, I stayed cocooned till my roommates had risen and stowed their bedrolls. Then I fled to the bathroom, where I stared in the mirror and swore I'd fight: "If they tell me to leave, I'll beg, I'll plead, I'll say I'll do *any*thing." I might have stayed all morning, if not for the frequent knocks, the yanks on the knob. Yielding my cave, I longed for a shroud to shut out the eyes.

Yet I still believed those eyes could be kind. When the meeting—from which I was barred—convened shortly before noon in the living room, I settled on a warm patch of grass in sight of the sliding doors and wondered what fix my friends might devise. Surely some revelation would rise to my rescue from the pool of group mind.

The doors slid open. Inside I saw an empty chair, facing Cayta. Lips in a grim line, she waved me to take it. I tugged at my circle-Z amulet; the string bit my neck. Cayta pulled her braid over her shoulder. My seat creaked as I leaned toward her.

"We think you should go," she said.

My head jerked back in shock. My resolve to stay snapped. A desert calm filled my chest.

"I think you're right," I said.

This was soul death. Yet I pulsed with life—which raised the question of how to survive in exile.

Packing to hitch to California, in search of a warmer winter, I recalled having left for Idaho with three hundred dollars' worth of ammo and a vow to return. This time, I might stay gone—and I knew desertion would haunt me. My best hope of relief lay in bringing no trace of the cause I'd betrayed—not even my circle-Z or *Book of Scriptures*. Unmarked, I could pretend I'd never been a Zendik.

But how would I get cash, without ammo, once I hit the road?

I knew Zendik pledged nothing to those who left. Yet Adam—who'd lived at the Farm a mere eight months—had received a $54 bus ticket, plus another $21. Shouldn't I get at least that much, after nearly five years?

For the first time, I felt Zendik owed me.

I found Cayta and asked for money.

"What do you need money for?"

To calm my fear, I thought. *To insert the slimmest buffer between me and the Deathculture.*

"Food?" I said.

She scowled. "I'll ask Arol."

Minutes later, she returned with $10—a slap, not a gift. A note inscribed, *See how little you mean.*

My one other request was a ride to the highway—ideally in the early afternoon, so I'd have plenty of time to find a kind driver who'd give me a place to sleep. With luck, I might even outrun the rain rolling in from the east.

Tough shit, I was told. Cayta would tack me on to her trip to get bread. We'd leave at five; I'd start hitching by twilight.

Around four, Arol descended from the master bedroom to her kitchen, hair gleaming silver against her purple robe. Seeking closure—plus a hint that she'd miss me? a sliver of hope?—I approached. My heart thumped, though I'd already plunged from her favor. Exile meant distance, not release.

"I just wanted to say goodbye to you," I said.

"Oh?" She turned to face me. "They decided you should go?"

Her show of ignorance might have perplexed me—had I been less obsessed with gaining one last shred of wisdom, or blessing.

"Yeah," I said.

She glanced at the sky, gray with rain clouds. "Oh well. Maybe you can develop your writing."

A scrap of hope, wrapped in despair. We both believed I'd fail at whatever I tried—art, friendship, love—without her guidance.

Yet into my pocket I'd slipped two white sheets, folded in quarters. On these, beyond her gaze, I would start my own story.

[chapter 14]

Release

I CLIMBED INTO THE CAB of Hunter's semi in the parking lot
of a Country Kitchen off Interstate 40 in western Tennessee.
His tractor, a sleek black Kenworth, had red and gold lightning
bolts shooting from the grille.

"*Mi casa es su casa*," he said with a wink, shooing Venus,
his black Lab puppy, off the front seat. She curled up behind a
gearstick high as my hip.

I met Hunter on September 29, two days after I left Zendik. By then I'd filled one white sheet with tugs, in tiny script,
at doom's grip: Might exile free the "I" trapped in "we," prove
that my time at the Farm belonged to me? Perhaps my task
now—since working harder hadn't worked—was to let go and
let life add to my list of Things I Was Out Here to Experience.
So far I'd enjoyed a night alone in a room of my own with a
door I could lock, and the kindness of a string of men driving
trucks. Hunter was the fourth trucker to pick me up.

"You can throw your bag in the back if you want." He
jabbed a thumb at the thick midnight-blue curtain dividing our
seats from the sleeper. The night before, I'd slept in a top bunk

in a cab trimmed with Christmas lights. I wondered if Hunter had one bunk or two. I knew he was due in LA Friday morning. It was already Wednesday afternoon. Maybe he'd drive all night and the question of sleeping arrangements wouldn't arise.

"That's okay. I'd rather keep it with me." I fastened my seat belt and stowed my pack at my feet.

Past Memphis, hurtling over the Mississippi, Hunter showed me photos of his two teenage daughters and his ring from the Virginia Military Institute. He'd served twelve years as a lieutenant in the naval reserve, he said, before buying the semi. His wife, back home in the Blue Ridge, was studying for a degree in pharmacy. He was giving me a ride, I decided, because he craved company and believed it his duty to help those in need. I grouped him with the born-again married man who'd driven me from Nebraska to Utah, my first time thumbing cross-country, and never once touched me.

I hoped Hunter wouldn't ask what I was doing on the road. When I'd tried to explain that to trucker number one, my voice had gone squeaky with sobs I couldn't stop. "I don't understand," he'd said. "It doesn't add up. You're crying like this over leaving your *friends*?" He'd sworn I was fleeing a lover who beat me.

Around midnight, we stopped to eat at an antiseptically perky roadside diner. I ordered bacon and eggs, crushing visions of caged pigs and chickens. For now, penury locked me in a toxic foodscape.

As I plucked the last fleck of egg white from my plate and started on the garnish—ornamental kale, an orange slice—Hunter asked, a teasing glint in his eye, if I knew what turned the sky blue. Rifling through my mental scrap heap, I snagged a tattered thought. *The sky reflects the sea, right? Or the sea reflects the sky?* I didn't know. But I wanted to. I noticed, as I groped for an answer, that I was flirting with him. He'd noticed, too. I saw it in his cocked head, his sly grin, his brows like furred rust, arched in expectation.

Back in the truck, he asked, "How are you at giving back rubs?"

I tensed. "Not so good," I said.

Letting go of the gear knob, he reached over and ran a finger down my spine. "It's this part that gets stiff from driving."

His touch left a tingle. I relaxed. Had I been too quick to deny a request as harmless as mine for a ride?

If concern for his wife surfaced, I dismissed it. Marriage was Deathculture bullshit—a mutual defense pact, masked as lasting love, that all couples, consciously or not, wanted out of.

Well past midnight, we crossed the line from Oklahoma to Texas. Hunter pulled off the highway at Texas Exit Zero.

He didn't say why he'd stopped. Maybe—despite the cigarettes and ginseng pills, the half-gallon thermos of coffee, my drive-all-night fantasy—he needed to sleep.

He killed the engine, then disappeared behind the curtain. Venus thumped her tail against the floor. "Come back here," he called. "I want to show you something."

What the hell does that mean? I thought. And then: *Maybe this is something else I'm out here to experience.*

Behind the curtain was just one double bunk, its mattress neatly sheathed in baby blue. Hunter sat, facing me, at the foot of the bed. "Lie down on your stomach," he said.

I buried my nose in a pillow reeking of aspen cologne. I felt his thumbs on my back, then his palms. The steady press of his powerful arms.

"Pull your shirt up. Undo your bra."

I tensed again. Had I shunned the role of Girl in *The Oraculum* only to take it on now?

"No. I don't want to."

But then his hands crept up toward my shoulders and over my breasts and my back arched into his heat. I ached for this. Doom released me, for a few delicious beats.

After, speeding west through a foggy dawn, I savored the gift of this night—coupling, for once, on my own recognizance. Could exile be wholly a curse and bear such luscious fruit?

Each week, Hunter drove round-trip, Virginia to California. I lodged at a hostel in Flagstaff, Arizona, and walked to the Little America truck stop every Thursday evening to ride with him to the coast and back. Saturday nights we bobtailed into downtown Flag to dine at San Felipe's Cantina or the Weatherford Hotel. Sometimes, after a couple drinks, I forgot my betrayal.

Between weekends I sought work, with scant luck. How to account for the gap in my résumé? I shied away from framing Zendik as a typical farm or artists' collective—and besides, I would have risked a bad review from any resident listed as a reference. Worse, I didn't *want* to wash dishes or bus tables or count cash for five or six dollars an hour. And I refused to gain a trade skill, as that would have meant investing in life beyond Zendik. So I scraped by on a couple money orders from my mother, the occasional twenty from Hunter, wages from day labor, and the kindness of a roommate, who paid for my bed at the hostel one night. I swung between panic and trust that I'd be all right.

One afternoon in early November, Hunter squinted into my future, the road ahead a haze of slate-blue rain. "I don't know what those people at that farm did to you, but I see a girl who's beautiful and intelligent and thinks she can't do anything. You need a plan for what you wanna do and how you're gonna do it."

I couldn't argue. Recalling that for a short time in North Carolina we'd thanked farmers beyond the Farm, in a grace before meals, I decided to try growing organic produce.

After vetting every entry in a national database of sustainable-ag jobs, I sought and landed an apprenticeship in Chico,

California, at Pyramid Farms. I'd get $7.50 an hour, plus a trailer to myself, rent-free, and all the veggies I could eat. I figured I'd save enough in one season to fund trips to the places succeeding Alaska and the Sawtooths in my travel dreams: Hawaii, Australia, New Zealand. Could razing my faith in a faraway Eden unbar my lost garden?

The job didn't start till mid-March. In mid-November, I moved to the Reevis Mountain School of Self-Reliance, a wilderness homestead east of Phoenix. I'd spent the month of August there in 1998 and returned for three weeks the following June. In 2004, joining four other interns, I found the scene both familiar and strange: *this* ring of young seekers 'round an older leader embraced me with appreciation and trust. As the orchard filled with persimmons smooth as pearlescent balloons and pomegranates like hives packed with jewels, how I saw myself softened and sweetened. Here I played a free woman bearing gifts—not a slave to unpayable debt.

In mid-December, I took a break from Reevis to meet Hunter for what he must have known would be our final ride. He'd burned his goodbye into the mix CD he handed me as I climbed down from his cab for the last time.

On the first track, a woman begged a stranger to remove her to parts unknown; on the last, a man wistfully released his companion to chase a dream of her own.

Months later, I burned the disc—watched it curl and melt— in a bid to break Hunter's hold. Grieving my loss, cursing his desertion, I couldn't dismiss our love as Deathculture bullshit. I did take solace in knowing he wouldn't keep me from Zendik.

At Pyramid, I worked mostly alone—fixing drip line, digging thistle, harvesting carrots and garlic. This freed me to design my days as I pleased. When summer's heat set in, I began rising in the half dark to start work at first light. Through by noon or one, I could read books, take naps, hunt fruit: kumquats, loquats, oranges, lemons, figs, cherries, peaches, plums.

But the joys of self-rule couldn't hold me on their own. As July marched by in a blaze of hundred-degree days, I grew surer and surer I was meant to be a Zendik warrior. The flour canister in my cupboard would soon hold enough cash for flights to my dreamlands. My fellow field hands—a couple sharing a trailer—wanted more space and more work. If I left, they'd get both.

Still. I expected quitting to cost me. In mid-July, gearing up to give two weeks' notice, I steeled myself for an angry blast.

Instead the farmer asked what he could do to help me beat the heat. Replace the cooler in my trailer? Build a canopy for shade?

But it wasn't the heat that drove me. It was my story. What he could change in that, he'd already changed.

In late August I set out overseas, hoping my Edens would disappoint me. Hawaii's Big Island dripped fruit (passion, bread, jack; avocados, sapotes, cherimoyas), as well as fresh coconuts, macheted for water and meat, but yielded no bohemian pocket I wished to slip into. New Zealand—backdrop to the *Lord of the Rings* films—withheld both elves and Rivendells. The Australian outback, richly embroidered with intricate song lines, seemed a vast, scrubby waste from the cab of a truck.

And yet when my jet touched down at JFK on October 7, 2005, I did not want to call the Farm. At rest at last in my mother's Brooklyn apartment, assured of shelter, food, and love, I dared to ask why.

Mostly I inquired in private, denying ammo to family and friends threatened by the revolution's critique of them. As for ex-Zendiks turned critics—*they* were lying whiners, dodging blame for their failures. Arol's voice in my head condemned them: "Get a life!" she'd say. "We're not perfect. Who is? But at least we're trying. Throw in or move on."

I had to shun such negativity, lest it infect me.

Thus the Zendik story sealed itself.

But not completely.

I met Sea through the blog I'd started in April 2005. She credited her few years at Zendik, in the late seventies and early eighties, with rousing sleeping gifts and blowing her mind. Yet she'd chosen, without regret, to settle elsewhere. In her first message to me, she said she knew the ache of leaving the Farm and treasured my giving it words. She assured me I could thrive in the outside world.

She slipped through the seal.

With her support, I raised my inner voice. Through October and November, I wrote and wrote, spreeing on thought crime (and bashing myself for it) as I spun strands of a new story:

I wished to live among equals, with reverence for each being's gifts and free circulation of feedback; I would not serve a hierarchy that lionized some, belittled many, and throttled dissent.

I wished to practice self-rule, based in self-trust. I cringed in rage, recalling all the times I'd sniveled and groveled in the face of accusation. Sure, I might have fucked up. But that didn't justify ritual humiliation or conviction in a puppet court deaf to my truth. Where was the compassion, the curiosity, that could have unmasked the plea beneath the trespass? Where was my care for myself? Why had I surrendered power to decide?

I wished to shed the weight of all-my-fault, the stain of cowardice. Maybe Cayta's judgment that I'd craved sexual assault had been neither true nor a move to empower me. Maybe I'd feared Arol because she'd roared, above the law of cause and effect; maybe I'd taken blame I hadn't earned because it beat risking soul death.

I wished never to sell again. I'd hated asserting my worth through numbers; competing with other sellers (while cursing my competitiveness); dodging them when I was bombing; waking in the morning, still exhausted, to the dread of getting blasted. Stripped of other ways to soar, I'd embraced running the money gauntlet as my highest art form.

I wished to tell my story as *my* story, not a footnote to Zendik's, in words dense and juicy as ripe fruit. I saw that my prose had grown more succulent, as I'd haltingly allowed *all* my flavors—bitter, tart, sweet—onto the page. I admitted that I'd often admired Zendik art only because admiration was required. Now I could freely seek art that moved me—and channel that which moved through me.

I wished to join all who were willing in building a beautiful world. As a Zendik, I'd believed our way of life so enticing that its popularity would one day explode. Yet in the year since I'd left, the Farm's head count had dropped to twenty-four. What did that mean for Ecolibrium? How would it grow, nursed by so few? Was Zendik pushing something the world *didn't* want? Maybe every act of beauty fostered beauty, no matter the source. Maybe Wulf, describing Ecolibrium, had drawn from a well I, too, could draw from, pouring what rang true into my own resurrection song. One thing I knew: in *my* Eden, we'd receive gifts and good wishes when we chose to move on.

I wished to claim my life as my own, with Zendik a stage in my growth. Wulf, urging flight from the Deathculture, had said, "Forget the old dream; save the dreamer." Had Zendik become the "old dream"? I saw I'd begun losing heart long before I'd left; had I *wanted* to flee but, fearing soul death, needed a shove? Could I be neither traitor nor failure, but creature achieving new form?

I wished to belong without condition. Once I'd lost utility, Zendik had dropped me. How could a human settle, and flourish, in a mesh full of holes? How could such a mesh be home? Why call the Farm, knowing no one there cared to hear my stories?

I wished to mate for life. I couldn't do that at Zendik, where, I admitted, I'd dropped men under duress. Maybe I'd marry after all; maybe marriage, when it lasted, strengthened the mesh.

Last—and most—I wished to go on loving *all* of those I loved. The Zendiks had pushed me from their ring to serve the revolution. But what if human ties were sacred and the world we yearned for hung on human ties? I would not snip links to family and friends for the prize of rejoining the ring.

But these epiphanies weren't enough. The threads I spun and pulled across my portal to the Farm formed a barrier no stronger than the hundred strands of fishing line I'd once snapped in one thrust.

I needed a weft for my warp, if it was to hold.

When Leah appeared at my door at 9:00 p.m. on December 1, she looked smaller and more vulnerable than the power seller I remembered. Her broad smile and warm hug held none of the judgment I'd half-expected.

I'd believed, since I'd left the Farm, that Leah's success on the street signified a faith far stronger than mine. So I'd been shocked, in April 2005, to see she'd vanished from the People section of the Zendik website. Surely, I told myself, she'd left on better terms than I had and would return before long; probably if I found her she'd shrink from the taint of my failure. But in mid-November, desperate to share my struggle with a peer, I tracked her down and made contact. It so happened she'd already scheduled a stopover in New York, on her way from San Francisco to Paris. Was she heading overseas, as I had, to mow down a fantasy? I didn't ask. We agreed to meet, not mentioning Zendik.

She wore a purple velour–lined jean jacket just like the one she'd spent hours adorning with free-form embroidery, in the van on the road. Her stitching spilled down the sleeves and around the collar, in shimmering whorls of turquoise, rose, magenta, gold.

After greeting my mother, Leah trailed me down the

stairs to the street. It was a warm night for late fall. We'd talk while walking.

As we climbed the slope to the park, my voice asked about Leah's travel plans while my heart pounded with fear of knowing and yearning to know—*would she return?*

"Yes" would shove me toward trying again and warn me not to blaspheme. "Maybe" would gain me a partner in confusion.

And "no"? Did I dare hope she'd say no?

A block up Twelfth Street, yearning won out.

"Leah, I have to ask: Do you think you'll go back?"

She stopped and turned to face me, the weight of the question pinning her to the pavement. "Can I be completely honest?"

My heart pounded harder. Maybe she, too, had fallen into thought crime.

"Of course! I wouldn't want anything else."

Her eyes sparked. Her spine straightened. In the glow of an overhead street lamp, the whorls on her jacket gleamed like dragon scales.

"I am *never* going back," she said.

My heart slammed against my breastbone. "Really?"

"Really. Helen, we went through *hell*. We're not bad people 'cause we couldn't make it there—it's one fucked-up place."

Thumpthumpthump.

"Wow. You know, I just recently realized *I* might not go back. Which was weird, because I thought I was finally ready; I'd worked out all these fantasies. But I didn't wanna make that phone call. I don't now. The thing is, though, some part of me still feels like I'm fucked if I stay out."

Leah turned and started up the block again. "When I left, I felt like shit. Like I'd fucked up the one thing that mattered. It wrecked me to think this was it."

I nodded. I knew the feeling.

"And then my dad sent me this book about cults. I was like, 'Whatever—the Farm's not a *cult*. People just say that 'cause they can't take the truth.' But I was curious, so I read it. And the way the guy describes cults—it gave me goose bumps. There was all this stuff that sounded *so* familiar."

"Yeah? Like what?"

"You know how Arol used to build us up and knock us down? One week you're her favorite; the next you're shit, you shouldn't even be a Zendik? Classic cult-leader crap. Keeps people off-balance."

"Okay." So Arol had *wanted* me anxious.

"That's the basic way a cult works. It's all about fear. You let people know they could be toast at any moment—and convince them they'll die, or at best have shit lives, 'out there'—and who's gonna fight you? They're all too scared."

I smiled. A fifty-pound sack slid from my shoulders, a fifty-pound disk from my chest. A thrill of lightness filled me. I'd been hauling both for years.

But what about mating? Surely Arol had accrued true wisdom, in that regard. Hadn't she and Swan formed the only lasting unions on the Farm?

"Did you notice," Leah asked, "how Arol and Swan *never* had to talk about their sex lives? *Never* got accused of being 'in a bubble' with their boyfriends?"

"Yeah, sure."

"Well, guess what? Maybe it's not so hard to get close to someone when you know you won't get slammed for it. How long do you think *their* relationships would have lasted if *they'd* taken the same shit *we* took?"

I pictured the Eye of Sauron table, in the dining hall in North Carolina; I imagined someone squinting at Arol and Prophet, then pouncing: "What's up with *those* two? They sleep together *every* night. They *never* bring themselves up. Seems like they need a break. Or maybe they should *get an apartment.*"

In the days after my breakthrough with Leah, I gloried in the gift of the world as it was. Yes, it brimmed with war, filth, glitz, lies—smothering warmth and beauty much of the time. But it was *vast*. And I was *in* it. Reminders of this—a dank gust from a subway tunnel, a block of dark chocolate savored while dancing down a crowded street, a goodbye kiss on my mother's cheek—unleashed waves of gratitude for my miraculous release.

Yet doubt still stabbed me: *Was I wrong? Do I have to go back?* My new story needed reinforcement. On the afternoon of December 15, I picked up the book Leah had read—*Combatting Cult Mind Control*, by Steven Hassan—and finished it by midnight.

Hassan starts with his own story: As a college student seeking a purpose purer than money and wondering if he'd ever find true love, he joined a group pledging ascent to a higher plane—the Moonies. For two years, he rose through the ranks, excelling at recruiting and fundraising, and inching closer to the group's leader, Sun Myung Moon. Seeing Moon as the Messiah, Hassan grew used to lying and manipulating in the name of world saving. He spent long days on the street, leading the Moonie version of Zendik selling trips (the Moonies hawked flowers, candles, candy, and other trifles for "donations"). On one trip—having forgone sleep to meet a sales quota—he dozed at the wheel and crashed the Moonie van into a tractor-trailer. He was rushed to the hospital with a broken leg.

It turned out to be a lucky break.

While he was immobile, his family brought in a team of deprogrammers—former Moonies who helped dissolve his cage from the inside while showing that those who'd left could be happy and whole. Later, grateful for the intervention but preferring a gentler approach, he developed exit counseling, which focused on coaxing the cult member to allow her inner voice to guide her out.

Reading Hassan's story, I laid my own experience over its contours and found a rough fit: After college, I, too, had been fumbling for something to believe in and stumbling in my quest for love. Zendik had promised elite status and a bump in evolution. Taking Arol as my savior, I'd skewed my moral compass to match hers. I'd exhausted myself hawking merch for the cause. Finally, a painful break had forced me toward escape.

Reading on, I added strand after strand to the weave of my freedom:

In a cult, the leader holds total control, crushing protest.

In a cult, the follower yields self-rule and self-trust.

In a cult, the follower is always at fault.

In a cult, the follower gives everything, denying herself.

In a cult, the follower receives the leader's words as sacred and uniquely pure, no matter how garbled they are.

In a cult, members take on the world's weight, assuming responsibility for human salvation.

In a cult, departure means death—of body, soul, or both.

In a cult, the follower belongs only so long as she serves.

In a cult, love for the leader trumps every other love.

In a cult, the follower must shun outsiders, lest they lure her from the fold.

Cult. Cult. Cult. In those shaky early days, I relied on the word, and the weave it completed, to block the gate to Zendik—a gate I could not yet block on my own.

Years later, I still see "cult" as the noun that best fits the Farm; a group's not a "commune" if one or two leaders control the money and own the land. But "cult" is a tricky term. Too often, it slices "us" from "them."

What *is* a cult? Dictionaries give bloodless definitions, like this one from my 1976 *Webster's New Collegiate*: "a religion regarded as unorthodox or spurious."

The heart of the word beats elsewhere.

In 1978, in the Guyana jungle, over nine hundred members of the People's Temple drank a deadly potion of cyanide-laced Flavor-Aid, on the last White Night. In 1993, in East Texas, eighty-two Branch Davidians died by fire and gunfire while resisting government intervention. In 1997, in Southern California, thirty-nine seekers of Heaven's Gate took lethal doses of phenobarbital and fastened plastic bags over their heads, expecting to wake on a spaceship.

In 1988, my sixth-grade class watched a TV special marking the tenth anniversary of the massacre at Jonestown. Did the producers ask who the dead were? How they'd found the People's Temple? What they'd hoped for when they'd joined? If so, the answers didn't stick. Nothing stuck but the heaps of corpses in lurid Technicolor—scenes from a horror film, misfiled in real life. No wonder I sealed that story and others like it in a pit marked "evil," "madness," "them."

In 2011, Julia Scheeres—herself a subject of religious violence—published *A Thousand Lives: The Untold Story of Hope, Deception, and Survival at Jonestown*. Drawing on sources such as a trove of recently declassified FBI documents, she showed that many entered the People's Temple seeking what life outside had so far denied them: comfort, camaraderie, the chance to serve what seemed a worthy cause. She showed how some fought to survive. She returned a throng of "them" to the ring of human understanding.

So what is a cult, again?

An IV of meaning and belonging for those near starving? A plywood platform for players lacking parts on the larger stage? A pack of soft animals lured behind bars by the dream of the warmth of a tribe?

All groups fall along a continuum, from reverence to contempt for self-trust. I find no bright line dividing cult from culture—just stories jointly held, and questions invited or forced by crisis:

How well do our stories nourish us?

What pain do we cause in their service?

How might we revise them—for healing, for kinship, for joy?

chapter 15

Reunion

EXACTLY *WHY* HAD I APPLIED for a job moving cargo by giant trike in the heart of Manhattan?

It was the morning of Friday, September 26, 2008—just one day short of the fourth anniversary of my flight from Zendik—and I was set to meet a prospective employer at his shop by Penn Station in a few hours. I'd all but decided not to show.

Once, in 1999, I'd biked from Park Slope to the far side of the Brooklyn Bridge. At the end of the promenade, I'd stopped, stared at the swarm of hulks I was supposed to share the road with, and turned tail for home.

I'd shrunk from city cycling ever since.

But I needed the money. And operating a vehicle so new to New York that I'd yet to spot one tickled my sense of adventure.

Plus, there was the save-the-world angle. The trikes, rated for loads of more than a quarter ton, could cut pollution and fossil-fuel use by shifting runs away from vans and trucks. Post-Zendik, I favored local action over visions of global renewal. Just a day earlier, I'd cheered the Yes Men as they dropped torn pillows, worn suits, and broken electronics at the rump of the Charging Bull, demanding government payments—commensurate with what the big banks would get, should TARP pass Congress—for their "troubled assets." Then I joined a mob at the Stock Exchange, chanting, "You broke it, you bought it! The bailout is bullshit!" In the midst of the protest, Gregg, the owner of the trike business, had called to arrange the interview.

I turned on my laptop and pulled up the company's website, hoping for a nudge toward yes or no.

I clicked from tab to tab, skimming text about pedicab sales and rentals, special-event shuttles, sightseeing tours, ad campaigns. No nudges there. Then, on the freight page, I noticed a small, grainy photograph of a man loading boxes into a cargo bay. I leaned in for a closer look. The man looked familiar. He looked like Jul—a fellow ex-Zendik.

Jul had moved to the Farm a couple years before me. Though he'd already achieved Kore status by the time I arrived, I'd known him to be humble and kind. I remembered how pleased he'd been, on a big demolition job, when my zeal for board sorting had freed him to tend other nodes in the flow from crowbar to truck. And I recalled a plea he'd made in a meeting, for a shift from ripping each other apart to appreciating our many strengths and contributions. (Arol, amused but unmoved, had urged him to go ahead and do all the appreciating he wanted—he could be the Farm's appreciator in chief.) Our tenures at the Farm had overlapped by about a year and a half; he'd left in 2001.

My eyes dropped to the faint gray caption beneath the image: "Julian Isaza, Director of Operations."

Yes, I'd keep my appointment. I wished to see Julian.

Within a few hours, we were sitting together, waiting for Gregg, in a nearly empty, dimly lit storefront across from a Lincoln Tunnel approach on West Thirty-First Street. The rickshaw company was moving here, from a space a few blocks away on Ninth Avenue.

Though Julian hadn't known of my application, he hadn't been astonished to see me. From my blog, he'd learned of my return to Brooklyn and my story of Zendik as cult—which didn't mesh with his respect for who he'd become in the Farm's crucible. He'd trusted our paths would cross at the right time.

He'd told me all this within moments of hugging me hello. Expecting Gregg any minute, we raced to catch up.

As my eyes adjusted to the low light, something tacked to the corkboard behind Julian's head came into focus and gave me a jolt. Something black, white, and all too familiar—a STOP BITCHING START A REVOLUTION bumper sticker. Nodding toward it, I asked Julian, with a hint of sarcasm, "Did you post that? To bring back the good old days?"

He swiveled to look at the corkboard. "No," he said. "That's Gregg's. He got it from some Zendik he met on the street." He smiled. "It's a perfect match, yeah?"

"It sure is." The business was called Revolution Rickshaws— RR for short. Or Revolution. Gregg had started Revolution.

From the rumble of his voice on the phone and my stereotypes about small-business owners, I'd formed a picture of Gregg that didn't flatter him: I saw a paunch straining against a stained button-down shirt, a bald spot poorly concealed by a comb-over, skin roughened and grayed by tumult and soot.

So I was surprised when Julian said, "Hi, Gregg!" to a trim, sturdy young man with pink cheeks and thick curls, stepping through the back door. He wore soccer flats, shorts, and a short-sleeved sports jersey. His shorts showed off his powerful quads and calves—a by-product of pedicabbing passengers around Midtown during the evening rush. Julian introduced me to him, mentioning our link through Zendik. Gregg wiped his fogged glasses on the hem of his shirt. "Welcome," he said.

As Gregg laid out the demands of the delivery job—hauling heavy loads through heat, cold, rain, and snow; handling aggressive motorists; negotiating pickups and drop-offs (notoriously tricky in Midtown office buildings)—Julian vouched for my grit and social skill. Couriers also needed to know the streets.

"Do you know your way around the city?" Gregg asked.

"Of course. I grew up here."

"Okay. How about if you come back Monday?" A veteran driver would train me to ride the trike in the RR parking lot; then Gregg would take me out for a road test.

On Monday afternoon, after I'd mastered the basics, Gregg glided through the gate on his Brompton, looking sharp in wingtips, slacks, and a dress shirt. He flipped the bike's rear wheel forward to park it and pulled out one of the pedicabs lined up along the fence. He hadn't worn shorts because he'd be in the passenger seat. I'd be driving.

Feigning calm, I pedaled, as directed, up Eighth Avenue to Thirty-Sixth Street and turned east.

"Now go back to Thirty-First."

"Does Broadway go south? Or should I take Seventh?"

"I thought you knew your way around," he said, teasing me for my I'm-a-New-Yorker arrogance.

"I do. But there's no such thing as a one-way sidewalk."

Back at RR, Gregg cleared me for the next step toward employment—filling out W-4 and I-9 forms at the old shop on Ninth Avenue. He released his bike from park and grabbed the handlebars. "I'll walk over with you."

On the way, one of us—probably me—brought up the bailout. A House vote on TARP had been set for that afternoon, and I'd adopted the view of writers on sites like Prison Planet and Blacklisted News that its true purpose was to speed the country toward tyranny by grabbing power for President Bush and his cabal. It *had* to fail.

At the shop, Gregg slid into a seat behind the office iMac

and pulled up a news article on the vote. "The House of Representatives rejected the bailout package, two-twenty-eight to two-oh-five," he read.

"Yes!" I said.

His eyes continued across the screen. "An hour later, President Bush and his entire cabinet were seen boarding a plane to Toronto."

"What? Really?"

A smile tugged at his mouth. His gaze stayed on the screen. "Bush said he feared for his life, now that his fascist ambitions had been exposed. A rotten tomato hit him in the back as he stepped through a metal detector."

The smile won out. When his eyes met mine, they twinkled with mischief.

"You're kidding," I said, smiling back.

"Yeah." He glanced down at the keyboard, in mock contrition. "I made up the part about the tomato."

That was the first time Gregg made me laugh.

In late October, a month into my stint at RR, Gregg—as president of the New York City Pedicab Owners' Association—received a couple dozen complimentary passes to a preview of Cirque du Soleil's *Wintuk*, at Madison Square Garden. Enticed by the promise of stunning acrobatics—if repelled by the holiday theme—I accepted his offer of a ticket. He paused to study the sheaf in his hand before picking one to give me.

I didn't realize till Gregg arrived, shortly before the show started, that he'd seated me next to him. For ninety minutes my eyes tracked the lead skater, swooping and leaping through a sleeping cityscape in his awful Christmas sweater—while every other sensor patrolled the few inches of armrest between Gregg and me. My skin tingled each time he leaned in to whisper a quip or a question.

Ten days later, we met for our first date—on a Friday night, in Times Square, at the close of the evening rush. When Gregg pulled up on his pedicab, I guessed from the shine in his eyes that riding gave him the same high I'd felt while selling. Getting fares took vigorous pitching; getting "on" meant wads of cash. Midtown seethed like Bourbon Street—with less piss and more plate glass.

We'd agreed to dine at an organic vegan restaurant on the Lower East Side. Gregg was sweating. I was fresh and rested.

"Get in," I said. "I'll drive."

After dinner, we cut over to the Hudson River Greenway and up to 125th Street, taking turns in the saddle. Driving, I savored the strength I'd gained making deliveries; resting, I relished Gregg's exuberance—and ogled his firm butt. A waxing moon dappled the river silver as the West Side Highway roared beside us.

Back at RR, after midnight, we parked the pedicab and moved toward the gate. Steps from the sidewalk, Gregg stopped. "How do you feel about kissing?" he asked.

"I like it," I said.

He grabbed my waist and pulled me into a lusty smooch. A motorist waiting for a green signal whooped his approval.

With that, we were off.

Shortly after New Year's, I traded my mother's two-bedroom for Gregg's Hell's Kitchen studio. The following October, Leah, now settled in San Francisco, paid a second visit to New York—this time with her boyfriend. She'd moved in with him before I'd met Gregg. Sharing a tiny table at a candlelit bistro, our mates at our sides, she and I raised our glasses to toast the two of them—and living *in an apartment.*

We stood at the front of the Great Room of the Old Stone House in Park Slope, about to take our vows. Sixty grown friends and family members, plus a number of their children, had gathered to witness our wedding. Among the guests were seven ex-Zendiks. Zeta, who'd explained how Zendik dating worked, who I'd sworn would never laugh again, was quickening the ritual with her violin.

It was October 8, 2011. Late afternoon. Gregg had proposed twenty months earlier, on Valentine's Day, saying, "Would you marry me?" I'd asked him to ask again, switching "will" for "would"; a wholehearted commitment didn't belong in the conditional mood. Now we faced each other, sharing the rug marking our "altar" with Gregg's best man, my sisters, and a British friend serving as "vicar."

Gregg spoke first, eyes moist with the risk of great trust—*I open to you; I drop my husk.*

Then it was my turn.

"I vow to tell the whole truth with love."

Writing life stories, I'd learned to see each feeling, each fact, as one node in a web of context. The more of my web I revealed, the more of his web I explored, the closer we'd come to communion.

"To nourish your good with all my heart."

In the front row sat my mother, beside her beau of two years. She'd walked me down the aisle. As I'd promised in my poem to her, I *had* found another way to be with men—modeled in part on her constancy. She had been there, tending my well-being, when Arol had not.

"To be with you and grow with you always."

That was it. Our vows were complete.

The vicar nodded to Gregg. "You may now lift the bride."

Gregg picked me up, spun me around, and set me down, to clapping and laughter.

Then—to gasps, and more clapping—*I* lifted *him* and spun him the other way.

Embraced by our tribe, we looped each other through an infinity sign.

Epilogue

IN SEPTEMBER 2007, SWAN married the man who'd fathered her third child. Soon after, Arol suffered a nervous breakdown. With Swan at the Farm's helm, monogamy became the norm. More Zendiks got married. Years after shying away from the sexy painter at Woodstock, Karma met her future husband while selling a Phish concert. Cayta married Taridon. Zar married a young woman who'd moved to the Farm in 2003, at seventeen.

In 2011, Arol's cancer recurred. She died, at seventy-three, on June 6, 2012.

By the time Arol died, Zendik comprised a dozen adults and a half-dozen children. After her death, hopes rose for a power shift. When Swan and her spouse dashed those hopes, half the adults left with their kids. Before long, the other four adults departed, and Swan put the Farm up for sale.

I count a number of ex-Zendiks among my dearest friends.

Vining through the ruins, human ties remain.

Gratitude

TO GERTRUDE GUNSET FOR "The Poison Tree," tears and silence, and the chance to apprentice to the craft of building sentences.

To Rebecca Faery for casting writing as a process of discovery. To Nina Kang for writing exquisitely, showing me "The Summer Day," and being there for over twenty years.

To the Dudley Co-op for a taste of belonging.

To Nancy Mitchnick for urging me toward the Gardner.

To the Gardner family for funds to launch my quest.

To my mother for succor, constancy, and always saying yes when I called collect.

To my sisters for keeping vigil and setting bold examples.

To my brother for holding the thread and smoothing my return.

To Gabriel and Celena Zacchai for reaching out and piercing my doom-cloud.

To Kyra Gordon for speeding my release.

To Steven Hassan for revealing the cult pattern.

To my early readers for turning the pages and telling me about them.

To my ex-Zendik comrades for turning the pile.

To Gary Bruder for the Vaio.

To Nancy Rawlinson for throwing me to the revision monster with the tools to take it on.

To Heather Sellers for *Chapter After Chapter*.

To Margaret Hollenbach for *Lost and Found: My Life in a Group Marriage Commune*.

To Katherine Burger, the Woodstock Guild, and my fellow residents, for four generative stays at Byrdcliffe.

To Dan Gilmore for preserving parts of my Zendik self.

To Verdant Nolan for lending me his archive.

To Jeanne Nolan for sharing her Zendik books and memories.

To Charles Eisenstein for thoughts on the nature of miracles and the power of stories.

To Louise DeSalvo for teaching me well and blessing my exit.

To Allison Hunter for asking, what's your book *about*?

To Lauren Frankel for buddying up with me and letting me peek behind the scenes.

To Medicine Wheel and Earthaven for abundant social nourishment.

To my 138 Kickstarter backers for helping provide my book-being with a body and a home.

To Michael Bluejay, Thomas McGuire, David Zukowski, Jerry Zukowski, Linda Zukowski, Edith P. Newman, and Gregg Zuman for Kickstarter superstardom.

To Brooke Warner, Cait Levin, Julie Metz, Annie Tucker, and the rest of the team at She Writes Press for partnering with me to produce a book I'm proud of.

To Gregg, my love, for our journey together and a nook of my own.

About the Author

HELEN ZUMAN is a tree-hugging dirt worshipper devoted to turning waste into food and the stinky guck of experience into fertile, fragrant prose. She holds a BA in Visual and Environmental Studies from Harvard and a Half-FA in memoir from Hunter College. Raised in Brooklyn, she lives with her husband in Beacon, NY and Black Mountain, NC. For more on life at and after Zendik, visit www.helenzuman.com.

Author photo © Gregg Zuman

SELECTED TITLES FROM SHE WRITES PRESS

She Writes Press is an independent publishing company founded to serve women writers everywhere. Visit us at www.shewritespress.com.

Fourteen: A Daughter's Memoir of Adventure, Sailing, and Survival by Leslie Johansen Nack. $16.95, 978-1-63152-941-2. A coming-of-age adventure story about a young girl who comes into her own power, fights back against abuse, becomes an accomplished sailor, and falls in love with the ocean and the natural world.

Uncovered: How I Left Hasidic Life and Finally Came Home by Leah Lax. $16.95, 978-1-63152-995-5. Drawn in by offers of refuge from her troubled family and promises of eternal love, Leah Lax becomes a Hasidic Jew—but ultimately, as a forty-something woman, comes to reject everything she has lived for three decades in order to be who she truly is.

Learning to Eat Along the Way by Margaret Bendet. $16.95, 978-1-63152-997-9. After interviewing an Indian holy man, newspaper reporter Margaret Bendet follows him in pursuit of enlightenment and ends up facing demons that were inside her all along.

Catching Homelessness: A Nurse's Story of Falling Through the Safety Net by Josephine Ensign. $16.95, 978-1-63152-117-1. The compelling true story of a nurse's work with—and passage through—homelessness.

The Coconut Latitudes: Secrets, Storms, and Survival in the Caribbean by Rita Gardner. $16.95, 978-1-63152-901-6. A haunting, lyrical memoir about a dysfunctional family's experiences in a reality far from the envisioned Eden—and the terrible cost of keeping secrets.

Pieces of Me: Rescuing My Kidnapped Daughters by Lizbeth Meredith. 978-1-63152-834-7. When her daughters are kidnapped and taken to Greece by their non-custodial father, single mom Lizbeth Meredith vows to bring them home—and give them a better childhood than her own.